Nigel Jepson is the author of two previously published novels, *The Inspector and the Superhead* (2000) and *Cut and Run* (Book Guild Publishing, 2006), each exploring the pressures facing Head Teachers in running challenging secondary schools.

As a Head Teacher himself, Nigel Jepson has successfully taken three schools out of Special Measures, two in Bradford and one in Rochdale. He is currently Principal at Kearsley Academy in Bolton.

By the same author:

The Inspector and the Superhead (2000)
Cut and Run, Book Guild Publishing (2006)

IN A LEAGUE OF HIS OWN

Nigel Jepson

Book Guild Publishing
Sussex, England

First published in Great Britain in 2011 by
The Book Guild Ltd
19 New Road
Brighton, BN1 1UF

Typeset in Baskerville by Ellipsis Books Ltd, Glasgow

Printed in Great Britain by
CPI Antony Rowe

A catalogue record for this book is available from The British Library.

ISBN 978 1 84624 599 2

1

'Football, did you say?'

As an experienced temp, Emily Lawson was used to all kinds of different work cropping up but a football club was a bit of a novelty.

'You're up for it then? Tessa's hard-sell approach never brooked hesitation. It was a big national agency and they expected you to jump. Just for good measure: 'Job starts tomorrow morning first thing.'

'Let me have a look in my diary, will you?' Emily held out, not wanting to feel completely on the end of a string. Then as an afterthought: 'How long would it be for?'

'Looks like three weeks but the Chairman of the Board at the club definitely needs someone who can start tomorrow. Someone on our books who is highly capable. That's why I thought of you, Emily, straight away.'

Oh not the flannel now! Sensing a slight desperation in the voice on the other end of the line, Emily suspected Tessa'd probably sounded out five or six other people already.

However, she didn't need to look in her diary to know she had no alternative work over the next three weeks. Was there really any purpose in holding out? Not when the money would come in so handy before the summer holidays. Perhaps Tessa was being truthful and she was the first person being contacted.

'I'll accept,' she replied almost perkily, before another kind of obvious afterthought sprang to mind. 'I don't suppose you could give me a bit more background?'

'Yes, it's Oakhill United Football Club.'

Emily indulged in a slight pause as she cudgelled her brain to check whether the name meant anything to her or not. It didn't. Secretly, she realised she had been hoping it might have been a big club in the north, like one of the Manchester teams or Liverpool or Everton . . . ones she'd heard of. Oh well, not to worry!

'Let me see,' Tessa went on, 'the Chair contacted me personally this morning only about half an hour ago . . . it all sounds very high-powered. The PA is on leave at the moment . . . happens they're hoping to make some kind of sudden Executive Manager appointment. Don't ask me what that means. The way the Chairman explained it didn't sound too clear but then I have to confess I've never exactly been an avid follower of the ins and out of football.'

'Make that two of us!' Emily echoed. If she was really being candid, football to her was twenty-two so-called grown men chasing a silly leather thing – or was it plastic now? Like headless chickens. But it was probably wiser not to spell things out too directly at this point, however much she might be preaching to the converted in Tessa.

'So anyway the Chair seems very keen to find someone to fill this executive post. There's a recruitment firm already involved called Greater Leadership Challenge – GLC for short. They're going to have a representative taking part in proceedings tomorrow.'

'Sounds very interesting!' Emily caught herself responding with a surprisingly sincere tone to her voice. For in truth it did promise to be a bit unusual, even if she hadn't heard of the team in question. Apparently it was in the Football League though. Just seeing behind the doors of a football club might be quite glamorous. It would also lift her street cred a good notch or two with her football-crazy nephew Tom.

'Oh! The other thing I need to tell you is that tomorrow's interviews or meetings – or whatever they are – aren't actually at the football club itself. They're taking place in a hired office at a chain hotel off a motorway junction roundabout. I'll email you the precise location and details later. Only the club is keen to keep media interest at bay. By the way, you're utterly sworn to secrecy until the process is over and an announcement has been made to the press. The club is aiming to do that by the end of the week.'

Not so glamorous then. But being top secret kept it sounding a bit special, even if she was a little disappointed she couldn't break her thrilling piece of news to anyone. Especially not to 14-year-old Tom who she knew would blurt it out to his schoolmates at the drop of a hat. Pity also that she didn't think she'd have the time to get her hair and nails done before tomorrow . . .

To Frank Borrow, the phone call completely out of the blue, from a firm called GLC about a managerial post, sounded too good to be true. Would he be willing to talk about it? Yes, he would. Then the man on the other end of the line, giving his name as Jonathan Woodhead, asked if Frank was able to make a meeting the next morning at a hotel somewhere in the north-west. Again, he agreed. Then this guy Woodhead said he would need to refer briefly back again to the Chairman of the Board of the club in question. Was it all right for him to get back in touch in half-an-hour's time for a longer chat on the phone? Frank said yes a third time. The phone call had lasted probably no more than sixty seconds. It left him in a bit of a daze but decidedly keen to resume the conversation!

His sudden hope was that now he might be able to put the last month's torture, since being sacked from his last club, behind him. During that time he had fallen prey to every possible kind of depressing thought about his future. He had tried as hard as he could to keep his confidence going even if it was just occasionally looking at the framed photos of the three winning championship teams he'd managed, photos which had pride of place up on his lounge wall. But even that was a mixed blessing because the soul-destroying message kept throbbing through his head that these successful memories and associations with the past might genuinely be just that, history.

At 62 Frank had convinced himself no-one would come looking for a man at his time of life. No matter how others might pay him the unsolicited compliment that he didn't look his age, he only knew he had begun to feel it. A month might not have seemed long on the face of it, but the anguished days of enforced idleness had begun to erode him inside. How many times, during the last wretched four weeks, had he re-lived that fateful last-minute goal in the relegation dog-fight game which had eventually put paid to his job? And how many times had he regretted not smacking the face of the Chairman of the Board as he had told Frank, with a gloating expression on his face, that he was 'relieved of his duties'?

Surely at his age, though, he should have known just how precarious was the thread that a football manager's job hangs by . . . that being sacked was a 'times-whatever' occupational hazard in this game. And, to be fair, as with anyone who had been a manager like himself for over 20 years, it wasn't as if it hadn't happened before. So why hadn't he been able to keep it in perspective? At times he had asked himself what was the point of going on. Only now, miraculously, there seemed to be some new hope to cling on to.

Forty minutes had passed. Frank glanced at the mobile phone lying on the table by his chair. Over the last four weeks it had gone entirely dead, to the point that it didn't seem to matter whether he'd kept it switched on or off. Another five minutes passed and Frank had almost persuaded himself it was an elaborate, cruel hoax being played on him.

Then, to his massive relief, the ring-tone started. Jumping up in his chair, he felt a sudden panic as if he might, through unfamiliarity, press the wrong button and do the unthinkable: cut off the caller. Thankfully, he heard the voice of Jonathan Woodhead.

'Is that you, Frank?'

'It is indeed!' Despite frayed nerves, he somehow mustered the strength of mind to sound ultra-confident.

Again, Jonathan's tone seemed warm and pleasant. More than

anything, it seemed he was keen to reassure Frank he knew all about his past career in football management. Tellingly, he made a special point of referring to Frank's three championship successes at unfashionable clubs. Jonathan even added that the club in question had specifically asked him to look for someone with a proven ability to haul teams up by their boot-straps. Then, almost as if it were a slip of the tongue, he identified the club in question as Oakhill United.

'Can't promise anything for definite though at this stage. All I can say, Frank, is that in the present circumstances they seem desperate to have a more experienced man in, like you, to support their current young manager who faces a hell of a daunting season ahead. Simon Steele is his name. For them to achieve their target of promotion out of League 2 by 2011, they know they need some extra managerial capacity!'

Glancing again at the photos on his wall later, Frank was aware of the coincidence of an exact eight-year interval between his major triumphs, all of which had been at different clubs. 1987 . . . 1995 . . . 2003 . . . no great grasp of mathematics was required to say the next year should read 2011. Before he even reached the club, he was determined in his own mind that the sequence should be maintained. He certainly wasn't inclined at this point to think of any hitch in his eight-year pattern of success.

Arnold Preston had been Chairman of the Board of Oakhill United Football Club for seven years and was very proud of the fact. In an era when big business had taken over virtually every other club in the whole Football League, he had single-handedly steered Oakhill United clear of any such stranglehold so that it remained what he fondly called a 'family club'. As a husband and a father, he had always sought to stay true to traditional values. He liked to think he operated as Chairman in the same way. Of course he recognised the importance of money coming into the club but hopefully by more orthodox means such as sponsorship and advertising rights. Believing in home-grown virtues, he had made it his central purpose never to let any outside-town business interest gain an overall control where it mattered, that is, in the boardroom. Apart from the local town hall, which he visited frequently in his capacity as a local councillor, the board-room of Oakhill United Football Club was the inner sanctum and focus of his life's work.

Even so, he'd been a politician long enough to know that you can't afford to let anyone, particularly voters, think you might be happy living in the past. Yes, he could remember with warm nostalgia the great Oakhill United team of the late 1960s, the team that missed out on promotion to the old Division 1 by the desperately slender margin of only two points. The dream of entertaining the likes of Best, Charlton and Law the following season had in the event been cruelly snatched away from them in the last heartbreaking game of the season. That of course had been the heyday of the club when his father had taken him to watch from the terraces. Football had been the religion of the town with gates of 30,000 or more. But, despite the fact that core support was now no more than 5,000 die-hard fans, Arnold Preston still believed he knew better than anyone else what made these modern-day supporters tick. Everything was based on a residual sense of loyalty. Win, lose or draw, you stuck with the team from the town of your birth!

Throughout the last twenty years or so, Oakhill United had found themselves stuck in the lowest league division – now euphemistically known as League 2. Promotion had always seemed a tantalising possibility with Matt Hewson at the helm as manager. In truth, the headhunting of Hewson, however pleased Arnold was for the manager himself, had come as a body blow to the club. In the meantime, they'd struggled for a year or so with two caretaker managers during which time they had failed to make a proper outside appointment.

Now the club had finally appointed a young man to the post, Simon Steele. It had to be conceded it was his first managerial post and results had remained stubbornly poor despite the manager's obvious determination to improve matters. The situation at the end of the previous season was that Oakhill United had finished up on its knees only three points above the bottom-placed team. It could not escape anyone's attention that, if this form continued into the next season, the club was in serious danger of doing an old-fashioned Accrington Stanley and falling through the trap-door into the wilderness of non-league football obscurity.

Despite tenaciously holding on to traditional values, Arnold was shrewd enough to see that Simon Steele, however promising, could not possibly yet have the necessary experience to deal with such a crisis situation on his own. Not that the Board regretted appointing Simon. It was just that the young man might need some extra support to tide him over the next few months. Personally, Arnold felt torn. He didn't want to make Simon feel in any way insecure, while recognising the need to tap into, hopefully for not too long, another manager's wider experience and track record.

In the end this had been the justification for the club calling in a similar firm to the one that had recruited Matt Hewson away from Oakhill United. Opposed to bringing in an outside firm, Arnold had made his views clear at the last board meeting. Usually whenever he spoke, it had the decisive effect of rallying other members onto his side. But this time the young Asian businessman Shazad Ali had spoken up passionately about the need to employ 21st-century recruitment techniques. A vote had been taken and Ali's proposal was backed on a majority count of hands. Despite all of this, Arnold remained desperately aware that having appointed Simon Steele to the post he had a duty to show loyalty to him. The man who might be brought in as Executive Manager had, in Arnold's view, to be committed to the continued nurturing of Simon Steele. Above all else, Arnold didn't want anyone coming into this post who might recklessly rock the boat. However important it was that the recruitment firm GLC came up with the right kind of person, Arnold felt his own, harder, job was going to be tackling Simon's reaction. After all, it was quite likely that the young man, having something of a proud nature, might be offended.

Didn't everything boil down to Arnold's own innate ability as Chairman to keep the Oakhill United Football Club show on the road? More than anything, he wasn't having GLC, or anyone else for that matter, telling him how to run his club!

2

Tessa had said 9 o'clock would be fine. Even so, Emily hadn't fancied best-guessing the early morning traffic. One thing and another, she'd ended up arriving at the hotel at eight.

Directed by the man on reception to the Hollingworth Suite, Emily was surprised to catch sight of somebody already there. A portly, balding, middle-aged man, in a rather well-worn jacket and open-necked shirt, greeted her in dignified fashion from the seat he was occupying at the head of the conference table.

'May I introduce myself? I'm Councillor Preston. Call me Arnold. I also happen for my sins to be Chairman of the Board of Oakhill United Football Club . . .' He paused as if to check the impact he was making so far. She smiled as graciously as she could by way of appreciation.

Then he launched into a potted history of the football club over the past one hundred years or so, before telling her all about his lifelong association with the local Labour Party. Football and politics – not her ideal mix by any means!

'You must be our saviour of a PA then,' he declared with the deductive powers of a Sherlock Holmes. She smiled inwardly at the thought – it must have been the agency dossier and the secretarial equipment that gave it away! 'Emily Lawson. Pleased to meet you,' she said, deciding to keep it simple.

With the opening formalities over, Councillor Preston now set out his stall to get on with business: 'I've a little typing job for you to do. Grab yourself a coffee, please do, and I'll run through it with you.'

The task entailed altering a sheet entitled 'Programme of Day', which currently bore a GLC letterheading the Chair wanted altering onto plain paper with one or two changes, including his own name and title on the bottom.

Just as she was on her way out to an ante-room to get on with the work, both of them were suddenly aware of thudding footsteps descending on them from the direction of the corridor. Then, almost immediately, the doorway was blocked by the presence of a bulky but fiercesome-looking figure in a tracksuit with the letters SS emblazoned on the chest. As if he had just come off an overnight training camp somewhere, his greasy hair was dishevelled and his pockmarked face unshaven. It certainly wasn't the exotic style of designer stubble she could recall seeing in the pages of fashion magazines!

Oblivious to Emily's presence, the man stood four-square staring at the Chairman like a dangerous, wounded animal. She noticed how narrow the set of his eyes was. His face was wild and disorientated. She had half-anticipated he would leap forward and bang his fist down on the table, bellowing out demands and grievances.

Instead, thankfully, he just about pulled himself together in time. The words he eventually came out with sounded highly respectful.

'Mr Chairman, do you think you could spare me some time?' His nerves were clearly on edge and he kept tugging down on his ill-fitting tracksuit top as a measure of his discontent.

To Arnold Preston's credit, he'd never flinched for a second. It was almost as if he had been expecting this bizarre episode.

'Now, Simon, that's quite all right,' he proffered in a calm, reassuring voice. 'But please just wait outside a moment. Then we can have a talk.'

Given the man's precarious-seeming state of mind, Emily wondered how he might react to being held in check one second further, but in the event he willingly complied and retreated out of the room almost subserviently.

On a nod from the Chairman, she herself withdrew to the ante-room. Much as she tried to concentrate on the task before her, the thin walls made it impossible not to overhear the ensuing exchange in the other room.

'But Councillor Preston, the players are bound to think it's a rum business having two bosses. Seriously, I think I deserve longer on my own to prove myself as manager. I know this guy is experienced but I'm the one who was appointed to the post . . .'

Eventually she heard the conference room door open and the tracksuited man emerge again. Somehow she had expected he would be wanting to leave with some final flourish or act of pique. But in the event it was the Chairman's voice which predominated, a subtle blend of command and cordiality.

'Simon, you've got to leave it to me to deal with the GLC man and keep this Borrow man in check.' Emily heard the voice of the Chair almost smooth-talking the younger man. 'Make sure you turn up in a calmer frame of mind for the meeting I've arranged at 11 o'clock. For your own sake and the good of the club!'

Automatically her attention switched back to the work she was doing altering the programme. While there was no reference to the meeting on the GLC version, it was set out on the Chair's amended copy. Out of natural curiosity she noted that those attending were: Arnold Preston (Chair), Jonathan Woodhead (GLC), Simon Steele (Manager), Frank Borrow.

It didn't need startling intuition on her part to work out that the man she had just encountered, with the letters SS on his tracksuit top, must be the manager Simon Steele. And she had naively been thinking that football managers only got excited about things that happened on the pitch!

'This guy you're recommending to us is hardly a spring chicken, is he?' were the very first words Emily heard Arnold Preston address to the representative from GLC. The Chairman had asked Emily to sit in on the different meetings and take notes.

11

She had half expected Jonathan Woodhead to be affronted by what sounded like a slight. But he merely smiled back as if it were a compliment.

'Yes, you'd certainly be buying into experience and a good track record if that's what you mean. But that's what you want, isn't it, to match up with the raw Steele?'

Jonathan Woodhead, with his navy blue sports blazer and shiny silver buttons, bore the hallmark qualities to Emily of a second-hand car salesman. Even down to the mannerism of emphasising the points he had made with a knowing wink of the eye.

'It's a case of opposites attract,' he continued. 'Think of the great double-acts in footballing history. Take Mercer and Allison at Man City or Clough and Taylor at Derby and Notts Forest. Pairs of men like chalk and cheese. But, in both cases, what a brilliant combination!'

Like a lawyer resting his case, Woodhead eased back in his chair, pausing to take a self-satisfied swig of the cup of tea Emily had made for him a quarter of an hour earlier. Trying hard to keep up with his fast patter as she scribbled away on her pad, his manner made her wish she'd slipped a tranquilliser into his brew. The Chairman, seeming to ponder a while on these two analogies, which had meant nothing to Emily, eventually said, 'Well, neither partnership ended up too happily.'

'But look at the success they had along the way,' Woodhead chirped back like a man with the ideal riposte for every question.

The Chairman paused again, thoughtfully. 'Yes just as long as The Professor understands our man is in charge . . . er . . . has the whip-hand with the players. Steele's the one the Board appointed.'

For a moment, Emily wondered who 'The Professor' was, although Woodhead not only seemed to know but smirked at the reference.

'The Professor knows football inside out. He's seen it at all levels. More than that, he's got the brains and maturity to know the right thing to do in any particular situation.'

'Hmm, we shall see . . .' the Chair muttered, clearly not wanting the other man to think he could be persuaded too easily. 'By the way, Emily, would you give Jonathan a copy of the revised programme?' And then, waiting to let him have a brief chance to run his eye over it, 'You'll see I've amended it a bit. Thought it only prudent to have Steele in as well. Otherwise he'd be likely to think things were going on behind his back. Have to confess I had a rather tricky conversation with him this morning. But I think he got the message in the end.'

For a moment Woodhead's confident manner slipped a bit. 'I alerted Frank to the fact there is a manager already in place. But I did tell him his post was as Executive Manager . . .'

A disapproving expression suddenly clouded the Chairman's brow. 'Well, it's up to me to decide how the two roles match up.' But then, as if not wishing to sound too brusque, he added in a more conciliatory tone of voice, 'I want you to know though, I think you've done well. If it looks like we have to have someone, this Frank Borrow sounds as near as dammit the kind of back-up man we'd want.'

Once again, Emily observed a gleam of self-satisfaction break out across Woodhead's face, as he took another draught of his tea.

'That's it then for our talk,' concluded the Chair. 'It's 11 o'clock now and I think time on the programme for the two other gentlemen in question to meet one another.' There was a keen, almost mischievous tone of expectation to his voice.

'Emily, will you do the honours and bring them in?'

Emily didn't need any second bidding. All this talk of 'The Professor' had sharpened her appetite as to what exactly Frank Borrow would be like. Simon Steele had already provided enough of a shock to the system. Now it seemed she was on the verge of encountering an egghead eccentric. She'd probably find him curled up somewhere on a sofa lost in a book on classical civilisation, panicking over being jolted back to modern-day reality . . .

Entering the room, Emily vainly looked round to catch sight of some similar manifestation of 'The Professor'. There were two men waiting there, both a little tense looking. One was instantly recognisable from earlier in the morning, appearing, if anything, even more ramshackle in his SS tracksuit. The other man was much older but almost suave-looking in a smart pin-striped brown suit with fashionable tie, shirt and shoes. Perhaps it was because she had been expecting someone much different that made it such a shock to her senses to see instead this tall, slim figure with a fullish head of hair rising to his feet in recognition of her arrival in the room. The agreeable smile on his handsome, tanned face, had her suddenly thinking that if he was really a professor, she would have been quite keen to enrol on one of his classes.

Simon Steele instantly reminded Frank Borrow of any number of truculent, abrasive 'senior pro' players he'd had to deal with over the years. Yet the last thing he wanted to appear, not on this first occasion at least, was confrontational. No, it occurred to him it would be a much better tactic to ignore the man's obvious attitude problem and set out to 'draw the sting' over a period of time.

Not that he hadn't already found the arrogant young man's demeanour highly provocative, to put it mildly. The time spent waiting with him in the room had offered enough of a foretaste. Shunning any civilities, Steele had pointedly ignored his offer of a handshake. He couldn't make it any clearer that he regarded the prospect of Frank joining the club as a threat, not a benefit. Once inside the conference room, Frank had hoped he would be given a chance to make some statement on his own behalf early on in proceedings, if only to try and reassure others present of his good intentions. However, the Chair embarked on a seemingly interminable act of oratory on the history and context of Oakhill United Football Club. During the course of twenty-five minutes, Frank had exchanged the occasional glance with Jonathan Woodhead. By contrast, Simon Steele was at pains to avoid possible eye contact with anyone and just sat there absorbing everything that was being said like a well-accustomed sponge. As far as Arnold Preston himself was concerned, he just seemed to take it for granted that rapt attention would be paid to his spell-binding delivery.

Just as Frank thought he was utterly losing the will to live, the Chair seemed, for no particular reason, to stop abruptly. With a piercing, almost evangelical look in his eye, he focused a question out of the blue in Frank's direction.

'Do you think it's a club you like, Mr Borrow?'

For someone who thought he had fairly fluent interview skills, the nature and timing of the question threw Frank completely off balance.

'Er . . . yes . . . but it's a bit difficult without having, er . . . first-hand knowledge of the club.'

To his mind it was the only answer he could rightly give at this moment, but somehow the Chair didn't look best pleased.

'So you're coming to join us, are you?' The Chair responded with what Frank had to assume was invitational intent. Out of the corner of his eye, he was momentarily distracted by the sight of Simon Steele squirming uncomfortably in his seat, venting his irritation by giving two or three pronounced downward tugs to his tracksuit top.

'Er . . . yes,' he responded. For a moment, Frank glanced round the table, perhaps hoping Jonathan Woodhead might have something to say. But he seemed content to sit there with a grin on his face like a cat with a tub of cream.

'That's it, then!' the Chair stated with an air of finality to his voice. Inappropriate as it may have been, Frank felt he had to interrupt at this point: 'Don't we at least need to talk over terms and conditions a bit?'

However, this provoked another look of indignation on the Chair's face.

'I believe, Jonathan, that's something you may wish to discuss further with your client outside.' The Chair seemed almost dismissive.

'Oh . . . yes,' the GLC representative piped up. 'Indeed!'

Rising from his chair, Frank still had a strange taste in his mouth. The meeting had finished rather too prematurely for his liking. Nevertheless he didn't want to sound a discordant note, so he dutifully followed Woodhead outside the room, leaving the other two men and the PA still sitting around the table.

Barely out of the room though, Frank heard Simon Steele give immediate vent: 'But Chair, who's going to be the boss? Him or me?'

'How many times do I have to say it, Simon. You'll be working together!'

'But I'm still worried about how the players will see it.'

'I'll explain it to the players myself!' the Chair concluded.

Frank's own meeting outside with Woodhead proved a very disappointing business.

'About terms and conditions, Frank, you'll need to negotiate with the club's financial officer to iron that side out. Think his name is Jack Hubbard. Sorry I can't stay longer. I have to be at a meeting in Stoke in half an hour's time. Must rush!'

Handing Frank his business card, Woodhead gave him one last knowing wink of the eye and turned on his heel out of the Hollingworth Suite.

'Good luck!' he shouted back over his shoulder.

Somehow Frank couldn't miss the message being spelt out to him. It was going to be his own responsibility to sort out any further actual details with the club. Well, if that was the case, he had better make the necessary contact with this Jack Hubbard fairly quickly.

3

Never too confident of her sense of direction, Emily was relieved to reach the road which led on to the housing estate she was looking for. Her handbag, lying next to her on the passenger seat, contained the keys to 8 Queen Anne's Way, the house owned by Oakhill United Football Club. At the same time, the thought involuntarily entered her head that she wouldn't like to live on this estate herself. She didn't think this was being snobbish. It just looked so grey and soulless. Not that the impression was helped by it being bin collection day. You could tell they'd been already because the emptied bins were scattered crazily all over the place, like coffins washed up on a barren shoreline. It was difficult enough negotiating the winding maze of roadways on the estate without the added hazard of a welter of black, blue and green nightmare obstacles littering the path.

Somehow Emily was reminded of her first day at work, a week ago. Probably it was because she hadn't seen Frank Borrow since that meeting at the hotel. She had been told he was travelling up today to view this house. Jack Hubbard had said for her to take the keys along for 10 o'clock, the time Frank was intending to get there.

Arriving rather too early, she was tempted to go in and view the narrow semi-detached residence herself. It looked so drab from the outside that 'tempted' was not quite the right word. More perhaps a case of filling in time. But she decided against it. After all, she wasn't an estate agent.

Whimsically she wondered how she would have described the

property to a potential client. Being honest, she would have to say: Character of property, dingy and horrible. Size of garden, smaller than a postage stamp. Design features of any interest: zilch. Probably, she wouldn't have made a very good estate agent.

According to Jack Hubbard it was Simon Steele who, just before going off on holiday, had suggested making this club accommodation available for Frank. At first she was impressed to hear of such a generous act of consideration on his part. But looking at it in the cold light of day, she couldn't be so sure of Simon Steele's motives. For some strange reason she recalled it being said that the best managerial duos were like chalk and cheese. If that were the case, Simon Steele and Frank Borrow should prove ultimate world-beaters!

Having been given the job of filing Frank Borrow's CV, she had delayed awhile and quietly taken the liberty of studying it in more detail. In particular, she was interested to find out why he had picked up the nickname 'The Professor'. Not only was it obvious he was well qualified, with a university degree in languages, but he had also acquired a master's degree in business administration. Hardly the average football manager! The degree in languages probably explained how he happened to have once managed a team in Italy. Emily was also intrigued to read how he had spent summers doing voluntary coaching in black townships in South Africa.

Just then she spotted in her rear-view mirror a car snaking its way down the close towards where she was parked. When it stopped, she recognised Frank Borrow, lean and tall as she could remember, climbing out. Feeling slightly doubtful as to how well he might recollect her, she got out to greet him, thinking she had better introduce herself again.

'Hello, I'm Emily Lawson . . .' She paused if only to spare herself any embarrassment if he wasn't able to place her.

'Delighted to meet you again, Emily!' he said warmly.

Instantly she experienced the same sense of reassurance in his presence that she had felt the week before.

'Did you find your way all right?' she thought it polite to ask.

'Yes although this estate is a bit er . . .' He looked round uncertainly.

As she waited, she only narrowly resisted the urge to finish his sentence for him. Er . . . grotesque?

'Confusing.'

She could sense he was straining hard to be polite. Anyone with any taste would take one look at the place and run a mile! Talking of taste, she couldn't help but think he made a good impression in his smart, fashionable top and designer jeans. She could definitely picture him holding his own in elegant Italian circles. The thought involuntarily crossed her mind, did he choose his own clothes or did someone else do it for him?

Pulling herself together, she had to decide what she was going to do with the house-keys in her possession. Dangling them in her hand, she speculated on whether he might expect her to carry out the job of opening up. The last thing she wanted to do was to appear pushy. Perhaps the most diplomatic thing would be just to hand them over and leave him to it.

'Since I've never seen this house before, I'm not sure that I can be of much use showing you around,' she blurted out candidly.

At least her remark made him laugh. 'Gosh, I'm very grateful for you taking the trouble to deliver the keys personally.' There was a slight ironic edge to his tone.

'Oh, no trouble!' She didn't like to say that Jack Hubbard had insisted she deliver them personally. That was ostensibly to stop the 'new man' dropping in at the club to pick them up for himself. All on the basis that Jack preferred the quiet life if he could possibly manage it.

'Well, here you are then.' She proffered the bunch of keys for him to take. She couldn't help picking up from the uncertainty of his manner that he might possibly feel offended. 'Oh I'm sorry, I didn't mean to appear rude just throwing the keys at you!'

'You didn't. But thank you once again. I know you must have a lot of work to be getting on with back at the club.'

Oh my god, she thought, even though he's being so nice and polite about it all, I think I've done the wrong thing. Deep down she would have preferred the chance to stay a bit longer. But now she'd blown it! Why did she always make problems for herself by unnecessarily complicating things?

Reversing her car, she snatched a last glimpse of him as he looked to see which was the key on the bunch that would open the front door. Quickly she retraced her way back down Queen Anne's Way and off the estate. The annoying thought came buzzing back into her head that he was now bound to think she was as difficult and unhelpful as all the rest of them at Oakhill United FC.

Inside the house, Frank Borrow took one look at the stark interior and wondered what the hell he was doing here. The smell of damp was rampant. The basic lack of furniture and fittings suggested bailiffs had stripped it bare. True, all he needed to do was politely decline the club's kind offer. If they were so keen to see him fixed up somewhere local, they might be prepared to put him up in a decent hotel until he could sort out a suitable property for himself.

But above all else, he needed to keep thinking positively. At least the torment of being out of work was over. His services were still in demand! Even if young Steele was likely to be murder to get along with, he was sure he was more than capable of looking after himself. Whenever he had started at a new club before, there had always been the inevitable range of issues to deal with. At least he had established with Jack Hubbard that he would be being paid on similar terms as at his previous club.

Standing in the cold, uninviting kitchen, and looking out of the back window upon desultory rows and rows of back-to-back houses, distanced from him only by a minuscule grass patch and a brittle-looking wooden fence, he told himself he was just going to have to put today down to experience. The thought crossed his mind that, if Emily had been willing to stay, at least he'd have been saved the effort of having to drop the keys off back at the club with a 'Thanks but no thanks'.

His thoughts were suddenly interrupted by a loud crashing which seemed to come from the front of the house. Moving quickly along the short corridor, he half expected to find the front door smashed through but thankfully it was still intact. Opening it warily, he took a cautious look outside but couldn't detect any major sign of damage or destruction. What he couldn't miss though was the incongruous sight of a black wheelie-bin crashed horizontally across the threshold. He wondered if it might be a strange initiation rite.

Then he heard the disconcerting sound of a shriek from somewhere, he reckoned down the side of the house. Suspecting it was possibly a prank being played on him by unruly youths with nothing better to do, he tiptoed round the front of the house and tentatively glanced down the narrow path which led on to the next semi-detached property to his right. But then his attention was caught by the sight of a red open-top sports car which was parked up twenty metres or so further towards the end of the close.

'So, so careless of me! I'm so, so sorry!'

Frank blinked at the sight of a young woman, probably in her mid 30s, with her back to him, appearing for all the world to be in fevered conversation with her car. At the same time, she was anxiously examining the bodywork. Then he could hear her exclaiming, 'Those wretched bins! How is anyone supposed to drive safely round this poxy estate! There ought to be a law forcing them to put them back properly.' Raising her sunglasses onto her forehead, she started inspecting the front wing in even finer detail. All the while, she seemed unaware of his presence. Given her apparent anxiety, he didn't care to risk startling her.

Just as he was thinking it might be better gently to retreat, she dramatically swivelled around. 'And I wholeheartedly beg your forgiveness for sending that wheelie-bin careering into your front door,' addressing him with an abject tone of apology in her voice.

21

She sounded like a guilty teenage reprobate in front of the head teacher. The earnest look on her face made him feel like laughing. But that would not have been appropriate at all. For there was something undeniably sweet-looking and endearing about her, almost a childish quality of wide-eyed innocence. Suddenly it seemed a bizarre situation he was in, feeling as though, by chance, down this obscure side-alley, he'd bumped into Holly Golightly and Sally Bowles rolled into one!

'By the way, who are you?' she put to him, with a kind of inquisitive air.

Again, the ingenuous nature of her utterance made him smile inwardly though his voice still somehow kept on deserting him.

'Oh, I must excuse myself again! That sounds much too direct and lacking in manners,' she said with a disarming tilt of her chin. 'My name is Rosie Skipton. I live here, well, over there.' She pointed two doors down. 'Rather wish I didn't but that's another story. Perhaps if you've got an hour or three!' She gave out a nervous giggle at her attempt at a joke.

'I'm Frank Borrow,' he finally found it in him to say.

'You're not anything to do with football, are you?' she said, before again remonstrating with herself: 'That must sound nosy! Don't feel you have to answer.'

'Well, yes . . .' he answered modestly, starting to be impressed by the apparent extent of her footballing knowledge. He didn't think he was well known to that extent outside the clubs he'd previously managed.

'No, it's just that I know the house you're in is owned by Oakhill United Football Club.' A bit of a letdown. Perhaps he wasn't so world famous after all.

'Only my son Ben is on the books of Oakhill United's Academy, or rather he was. The guy who ran the team used to live in that house. Ben was terribly sad when Andy left the club a year ago. The new manager dropped Ben out of the Academy. Terrible man! Ben was picked on.'

Frank listened on sympathetically as her tone suddenly changed to sad and almost angry. He was hoping he would get the chance to tell her he was the new Executive Manager of the club, but the right moment never happened. Instead, he referred back to her mention of the club's house. 'It doesn't look as if anyone's been living here recently,' he said. 'You can tell from the damp.'

She was still too engrossed in her son, though. 'Ben used to like going round to see Andy. I think he became a kind of substitute father-figure to him. In fact, I swear several of my CDs and DVDs ended up being left in that house.'

Then, as if something else had sprung into her mind, she shot an agitated glance at her watch and let out another little shriek. 'Oh, is that the time? I've got to be at the blood donor centre! Must rush . . . by the way, it's been very nice talking to you, perhaps another time?'

At the same time as reflecting on the fact she was probably a nurse by occupation, he nodded back, appreciating she hadn't needed to say what she had done at the end. He couldn't deny it had been an unusual and very much unexpected encounter.

Returning to the house, having placed the number 8 wheelie-bin in a safer place round the back, he juggled the bunch of keys in his hand. The decision to return them to the club today had been a no-brainer twenty minutes ago. Trying to work out why he was not feeling so certain now, he couldn't quite pin the reason down. But with this scheduled short trip to Italy ahead of him, it just seemed wiser to leave all possible options open for the time being, and defer making a decision until he got back home.

4

Frank glanced at his watch and saw there was still half an hour in hand before the meeting. He knew the area well enough to be aware he was only five minutes walking distance from the Bar Palio.

He had made his way to Siena from the hotel where he had been staying the last two nights and parked his rental car on a lot outside the city walls. Trudging up the steep medieval streets, he had eventually caught sight of the towering landmark of the black and white duomo. Knowing it was lethal hanging around too long under the boiling midday sun, he had bided his time by taking a cappuccino in a shaded, backstreet café.

Surprised at how nervous he was feeling, he tried convincing himself there was no logical reason for it. Hadn't he spent the whole of the outward plane journey rehearsing precisely what he needed to say to Carla? At least she had agreed to meet him on his own this time. On recent visits such a thing had proved impossible. In characteristic fashion she was always surrounded mob-handed by members of her extended family, as if needing protection from the errant ways of her absentee husband.

This time he had texted her in advance to see if the two of them couldn't meet up for a private talk. In hindsight, however, it might perhaps have been wiser to suggest holding the meeting somewhere a bit less frenetic than the familiar tourist-trap of the central Piazza del Campo. Fidgeting nervously with a spoon, he indulged himself by stirring an extra sugar into his drink. To keep himself calm he reminded himself he would be catching a plane back home later that evening. Added to that, the short visit here came at a good time, knowing he had a job to do at Oakhill United. Not that he didn't have an abiding fondness for the city of Siena. Perhaps, if he ever came back again, he might just be able to enjoy its pleasant atmosphere without other practical matters weighing so heavily on his mind.

Thinking back, Siena had seemed a veritable paradise at that stage of his managerial career in the mid-1990s when he had embarked on an almost unique switch from being a manager in England to an equivalent *allenatore* in Italy. Heralded at the time as a revolutionary undertaking for an English manager, it had been a huge challenge, not least linguistically. His command of Italian, which he had picked up at university and reinforced as a school teacher while playing semi-pro football and then taking up coaching, had enabled him to feel confident about transcending the cultural barriers that might have stood in his way.

One immediate unfortunate consequence, however, had been the breakdown of his marriage to Penny. Although pleased for him initially, she had never seemed keen on making the move herself. At the time, he could understand why. While everything admittedly had been fine for him, Penny must have felt like a prisoner having to struggle with the feeling of isolation in an unfamiliar, foreign setting. Although he had no real option himself but to continue, she had eventually returned to England. To her credit she had never blamed him for acting selfishly although he recognised she would have been within her rights to do so. But as soon as it was agreed she would return to England and he would stay on, the die had seemed inevitably cast. Then, soon after, he had met Carla and everything had led on to his even fuller immersion into Italian life. Courting a younger signorina seemed to have a remarkably rejuvenating effect on him. As his team went from strength to strength, so his own prospects flourished. He and Carla had become man and wife at a wedding ceremony in Siena.

As if to further demonstrate how cruel fate could be, despite three good years, new owners had taken over the club. Politics being what they were, they of course had wanted their own man in charge. However well the team was doing, he knew from that point on his days were numbered. In the end he had been replaced by a man of impeccable Tuscan descent.

Frank had never thought his second marriage would go the same way as his first, but unfortunately it did. Needing to find an alternative job back in England, a similar situation occurred only in reverse, this time with Carla finding it impossible to adapt to life in a different country. Four years ago they had agreed on a separation, but their marriage had remained in that suspended state in the meantime.

Trying his hardest to resist pangs of agitation rising up inside, Frank took another anxious look at his watch and saw there were still ten minutes to go. Above all else, he told himself to stay level-headed. It was vital he didn't allow thoughts from the past to unsettle him. For this reason he needed to shut all those memories out of his mind and concentrate purely and simply on the basic business he had come to Siena to carry out. That in essence was to convince Carla to agree to switching from separation to outright divorce. Although he believed that, for different reasons, she might still be opposed to this more formal undertaking, he had to try his utmost to persuade her it was the best thing for them to agree to.

Slowly, he rose from his chair, settled up with the barista and shuffled back out again into the scorching sunlight.

From the very start that Monday morning, Emily thought that Jack Hubbard had been acting strangely out of character. For one thing, he was already in his office before Emily arrived when usually he didn't roll up until mid-morning. Instead of his customary lethargic demeanour, he seemed like a man possessed.

In contrast to the philosophical, almost vacant, expression on his face that she had become accustomed to in such a short space of time, his brow bore a worried frown.

Normally, at the start of each day, Jack's habit was to distract her for at least a quarter of an hour with some leisurely critique of a TV programme he might have been watching the night before. This could be irritating when she had to switch her mind off work, even if she charitably put it down to it being the time of year when things were not quite so busy in the office.

It didn't call for extraordinary powers of perception on her part to see that today was different. It looked like the building had been burgled and the office ransacked. Box-files lay gaping wide open, spreadeagled on tables with pieces of paper strewn all over the place.

She caught half sight of a man staring bereft at a computer screen in his office space. She couldn't think it was Jack, but she was wrong. Something completely novel about the whole scenario made her feel an immediate instinct to go and check that everything was all right with him.

'It's nothing,' was all Jack said with his practised deadpan style of delivery. But despite not looking up from his screen, she could see he was sweating profusely.

'Is there anything I can do to help?' She thought she had better make an offer.

'Er . . . no . . .'

She still didn't quite know how best to respond, never having seen him look so concerned and preoccupied before. Perhaps she had better just take him at his word and leave him to get on with what he thought he had to do.

Then, as though relenting, Jack looked up and said to her in a kind of conspiratorial whisper, 'The Chairman of the Board rang me last night to say he would be coming in this morning at 9.30.'

Not at all sure what significance this might have, Emily was again at a loss to know how to respond.

'. . . To talk to me about the desperate state of the finances.'

The heavy emphasis on the last few words clearly suggested these had been the Chairman's own words.

Involuntarily, she checked her watch. Catching sight of this, he shook his head. 'Yes, only fifteen minutes to meltdown!'

'Is the meeting with the Chair in your office?' she asked, casually letting her eye wander from his office through to the other area. She was really just trying to alert him to the adverse impression it might create if the place looked such a tip.

'Yes, of course,' he clocked. 'I'm going to have to clear the place pretty quickly, aren't I? Can't have it looking like a bomb's been dropped, can we?'

'Can I help?' she tried a second time.

But again he resisted stubbornly. 'No, there's only me knows where to put things.'

She smiled uncertainly back, accepting it seemed there was little she could do. During the time remaining, she was uncomfortably conscious that he just appeared to be throwing papers back in boxes any old how. It was hardly reassuring, even though the area might not now look quite so chaotic when the Chairman arrived. On Jack's behalf, Emily was only grateful Arnold Preston hadn't arrived early for his meeting.

When he did arrive, sharp on 9.30, he could have been forgiven for thinking the place was its usual haven of apparent peace and good order.

Doing her best to present a professional front-of-house image, she smiled but was somewhat taken aback to hear him say to her in passing, 'Oh and remind me, I need to have a quick word with you after my meeting with our Director of Finance.'

For the next half-hour, trying her best to keep her mind occupied on other things, she still wondered what on earth it could be about.

Eventually, the Chair emerged from the inner office after his talk with Jack. Although she felt understandably curious as to how this had gone, by now she was far more anxious about what it was he wanted to say to her.

'You asked me to remind you . . .' she gently sought to nudge his memory.

'Yes certainly I remember, I wanted to say something to you, didn't I?' the Chair said with what sounded to Emily an ominously significant air. Either he was winding her up on purpose or perhaps he was genuinely unsure how to proceed. But after a further suspenseful pause, he merely said, 'I think it's probably better if you ring the agency yourself. Someone called Tessa, isn't it?'

With that, he was off on his way again.

Dying to ring Tessa straight away, she first had to listen to Jack's post-mortem: 'We've got the auditors coming in. For auditors, read the Spanish Inquisition, I can tell you! I swear it's all because of taking on this 'new man' Borrow. I shouldn't say this to you but it's going to throw up a hell of a lot of problems. The Board are bringing in some auditor firm to come up with a range of ways the club can make cuts or savings.' And then with an almost paranoid twitch of his lips, 'It seems I'm not to be trusted!'

'Oh?' was all she could muster in response, not wanting to offer him too much leeway to continue.

'Well, I suppose I ought to get on with things again now,' he thankfully concluded.

Pouncing on the phone, she instantly contacted Tessa.

'Hello Emily. You'll be pleased to know the club says it wants to keep you on.'

'But the PA's due back off leave at the end of this week?' she protested.

'Not sure! Reading between the lines, it sounds like the lady in question has done a runner with the ex-manager, by the name of Hewson, and won't be coming back. Between the two of us, fishy goings-on at that club!'

'Where does that leave me then?' Emily felt the need to probe further.

'Obviously, as things stand, the placement is now going to be for rather more than the original three weeks . . . if you're agreeable, that is.'

'What would you advise me to do?'

'Well, first of all be careful about relationships with managers!

No, all joking apart, for the time being at least I think it's going to be a case of taking things one week at a time at Oakhill United.'

'So just to continue then?'

'That would be my advice.'

Climbing down the last few steps and passing through a narrow gateway into the Piazza del Campo, Frank felt as always on making the entrance, like a gladiator entering an amphitheatre. In more prosaic footballing terms, it was a similar nerve-tingling sensation to emerging in the blink of an eye from the cocooned warmth of the changing rooms into the brilliant, blinding lights of a floodlit stadium.

However many times he had previously ventured into the Piazza del Campo, and despite how very tense he might have been feeling today, he still experienced the same thrill as ever to his senses. Regardless of the countless hundreds of others thronging the piazza, his eyes shot up instantly in hypnotised fashion to the startlingly bright walls of the town hall, known as the Palazzo Pubblico, adjacent to the incredible bell tower that jutted up imperiously into its pure azure frame of a skyline.

Desperately he tried to protect his fragile sense of equilibrium by shielding his eyes from the magnetic distraction of the setting. His efforts were in no way assisted by the supreme irony dawning on him, belatedly, that the Palazzo Pubblico was where he and Carla had not so many years ago fervently exchanged their marriage vows.

Doing his best to assume an air of studied composure, he kept close to the gateway. At least it would give him a chance to scan the wide, serried ranks of tables and chairs at the Bar Palio to check if Carla might have arrived already. Failing to spot any single woman on her own, he decided to wander over to claim a table and await her arrival in due course.

'Franco! Franco!' He suddenly heard his name being called out. Because it was discernibly a man's voice doing the shouting, he didn't at first take too much notice.

'Franco! Over here!'

Looking round, his attention was drawn to the sight of two people, a woman and man, sitting together at a table at the far edge of the café. Rubbing his eyes for a second, he identified Carla and her younger brother Marco.

'*Buon giorno, Franco! Comé sta?*' Marco started gushing on his approach, grabbing onto him like a long-lost brother. Meanwhile, Carla remained motionless.

'What would you like? *Una birra* for the Englishman?' For a gatecrasher, Marco was certainly working his ticket.

Frank wasn't going to argue and merely nodded his head to the offer. Deliberately, he then fell silent. Adopting a similar manner to that of Carla, he slipped lower into his chair and just nonchalantly sat there eyeing up passers-by in accepted passeggiata mode.

The waiter took their orders in due course and, in advance of the drinks, left a bowl of peanuts. Marco offered them round before guzzling a handful himself. There was enough general bustle and activity going on for the combined silence between the three of them not to seem too strained for the time being.

To keep his mind occupied, Frank tried working out how old Marco must be by now. As the younger of the two brothers, he was probably in his mid-30s. When he was the manager at Siena, Frank remembered how as a teenager the fawning Marco had been as sweet as pie when wanting tickets for a match for himself and his gang of mates. Perhaps if only to curry favour with his elder sister, Frank had invariably complied by providing tickets for the VIP enclosure.

Finally the waiter arrived with a shining, silvery tray bearing a campari for Carla, a tall beer for himself, and an orange spremuta for Marco.

'Well, bottoms up as you say in England!' Again, as far as Frank was concerned, the show of conviviality fell on deaf ears.

Some instinct in Frank made him feel as though he needed to take greater charge of the situation.

'Why did you bring Marco with you?' he expressed directly to

Carla. Naturally he hoped she would give an answer herself, but she only lowered her eyes like a stubborn schoolgirl and it was Marco who responded.

'Look, my brother,' he appealed with an expansive shrug of his shoulders. It was the kind of gesture Frank had so often seen routinely given by Italian footballers to referees after committing a stealthy foul. Marco's face had protesting innocence written all over it.

'For one thing, I am not your brother!' Frank wanted to make it absolutely clear. 'Second point is, I addressed my question to Carla!'

The next moment Marco's face bore the injured look of a player reacting indignantly to the unjust handing out of a yellow card.

Brother and sister then exchanged mutually sympathetic glances. Frank realised yet again the need to take into account that blood was thicker than water. Particularly in these parts.

'I'm sorry, but just for once . . .' he openly appealed to Carla. 'I thought we were going to be able to talk together on our own.'

Without any warning, she collapsed into tears. Marco protectively put his arm round her shoulders while Frank was left looking round in embarrassment as people at neighbouring tables watched with more than usual interest.

'Franco! Franco! Carla asked me to come along because she was . . . how do you say? Scared you would be angry at what she wanted to tell you!' Marco put to him, at the same time glancing appealingly in the direction of his sister.

'So what is it you want to tell me?' Frank rasped impatiently.

'Look, Franco, I do not feel easy in saying this . . .' Marco began, 'but you and Carla have not been "man and wife" for years now. *Vero*? It is true, is it not?'

Excruciatingly, conversation on neighbouring tables came to a complete standstill.

'Er . . .' Frank felt distinctly reluctant to commit himself for the moment.

'Well, I have to tell you Franco, that Carla has met a young man from Volterra.'

What was this, if not public humiliation?

'Yes and . . .' he found himself provoking Marco to come to the point.

'Carla and our whole family feel it only right that the two of you seek a divorce settlement.'

'So what would you like me to say in response?' Frank's gaze veered erratically between Carla and her prosecuting advocate of a brother.

'That you are in agreement with a Siena law firm being contacted to draw up all the necessary legal papers.'

'Indeed I am!' Frank complied almost sheepishly. Somehow, in accepting so willingly, he couldn't help feeling he had been wrong-footed throughout, a complete victim of Latin guile. Even if he was now set to return to England with roughly what he had come out here to achieve in the first place, it still left him with a curious, sour aftertaste.

Like an animal retreating, tail between legs, he made his way out of the piazza through into the tight, surrounding passage-ways that would lead him back down beyond the city walls to the car park. The only slight detour he allowed himself, for sheer nostalgia's sake, was to catch sight of the football stadio.

Now there was nothing to detain him before he hit the autostrada. In good time to reach Pisa airport, he thought of stopping on the outskirts of the city at a ristorante where the Sienese club had celebrated one night after a famous away victory in the Coppa Dell'Italia. But dismissing it as pointless self-indul-gence, he decided against and drove on.

With the CD blasting out his favourite arias from Italian operas, he recalled how he played the music at full volume in the changing room to rouse his team before the start of a game. In the mood he was in at that moment, he could only hope it would have a similar effect on his own spirits.

5

Frank wiped the sleep from his eyes and, in shock, noted the time on his bedside clock: 9.43. By anyone's standards, let alone his own exacting ones, this was late to be waking up.

The flight from Italy back to Manchester the night before had been delayed and he hadn't got home until after midnight. But that wasn't the real issue. Despite his late hour of return, he hadn't been able to switch off from the visit to Siena and had felt like winding down with a drink or two. That had only been the start of it though. Disastrously, in the end, the two fine vintage bottles of Brunello that had travelled back with him from his favourite vineyard outlet in Montalcino had been drained dry, as he had sunk deeper and deeper into a self-indulgent stupor. Around 3 o'clock in the morning, he could vaguely recall crawling paralytically up to bed.

Apart from leaving him with a painfully thick head now, the other nasty consequence was the flagrant waste of finest wine. His more discriminating tastebuds had died a death by roughly a quarter way through the first bottle. From that point onwards, it could have been any old supermarket plonk shooting down his neck.

The trouble was that the antics of that smart-ass Marco had really got to him. He had needed to consume that amount of wine to rid himself of the memory of what still seemed like a staged humiliation. He didn't blame Carla. After all, her presence had been almost irrelevant. For some strange reason, what

34

had piqued him most was the description of the man from Volterra as 'young'. Whatever 'young' was, it was meant as a telling reference to the twenty-year age difference between himself and Carla. On the plane back, it had occurred to him that Volterra was the place with the museum of Etruscan stickmen. Surely there was some clever remark he could have made in that context? But it was rather late to be thinking about it now. Far too late.

Driven by his conscience to crank himself up from the mattress, Frank slipped a dressing-gown over his shoulders and stumbled out of his bedroom. On the top floor of the narrow three-storey house, he had to take extra care negotiating the two flights of steep stairs. In his state he could easily have fallen headlong. It wouldn't make a good start for the season ahead to be attending the first training session on crutches!

Still in one piece at the end of the treacherous descent, he arrived in the kitchen, only to catch recriminating sight of the two emptied bottles of Brunello standing side-by-side like forlorn war victims at the back door. Not feeling like touching food, he poured himself a tumbler of cold water and gulped it down in one draught.

Mooching down the corridor, he opened the curtain across the front door to let the morning light in and noticed an object lying there which had obviously been slipped through the letterbox. It looked like a DVD or CD container. He could see a handwritten note in black biro attached which read:

> As new Executive Manager of the club I thought you might like to see this!
> Best Wishes Ben Skipton
> By the way, I only live down the road at 3 Queens Anne's Way.

Despite his delicate state, Frank felt able to work out this must be the son of the young woman with the red sports car he'd encountered. He'd obviously been doing his detective work to find out who Frank was. On closer inspection, the DVD itself had a line written across it: 'Oakhill United v Rochdale April 2010 SKY'.

Given that he knew so very little about the team and its players at this stage, Frank could see it was a useful as well as a thoughtful gesture on the part of the young lad. It occurred to him that it could be just the thing to distract him from the Italian experience and might even help clear his head.

Taking the DVD back upstairs with him to the lounge, he slotted it into the TV and lolled back on the settee to view his new team at leisure. Two minutes in, however, he was sitting bolt upright like a passenger in an aeroplane during a shaky take-off. As the ball rattled against the Oakhill United crossbar, he was not sure he was so grateful to Ben for the loan of this X-certificate DVD after all!

By twenty minutes in, Oakhill United are still playing like novices and a goal down. Then they concede a second, a simple header from a corner with the scorer completely unmarked. The ball in the back of the net, Oakhill United defenders glare at each other accusingly. As the away team excitedly hug one another, the camera pans to the touchline to pick up Oakhill United's manager, Simon Steele, going ballistic. Frantically he is tugging his tracksuit top down in trademark manner. Nor do you have to be a lip-reader to know what kind of utterances he is making from his technical area.

Frank had no idea what the final score was going to be. All he did know, at this point in viewing, was that his headache was growing worse by the minute. The idea of this team winning the championship was unthinkable.

Suddenly Frank heard the doorbell go. Hearing it was almost like the relief a boxer feels hearing the bell at the end of a bruising round. However, wearing only his dressing-gown and in unshaven state, he decided against responding. It went a second time. Still determined not to answer, he took a snatched look from the upstairs window. On the doorstep, he caught sight of a boy, probably no more than sixteen. Withdrawing, Frank waited a minute or two before checking again. Fortunately this time, the boy had gone. Standing back a little from the window, Frank was able to follow the boy's path as he crossed the road and then retreated into a house not far away on the opposite side of the street, which was, if he was not mistaken, 3 Queen Anne's Way.

Frank was going to have to be on his mettle, wasn't he? Ben Skipton already seemed to be very much on his case.

'Seven hundred! Only seven hundred!' Arnold Preston vented his disbelief on Jack Hubbard.

It looked like another bad meeting ahead, the thought occurred ominously to Jack. 'Afraid so, Chairman.' Then unhappily: 'I admit it doesn't look good.'

'Doesn't look good? Understatement of the year, Jack! Or, for that matter, any other year . . . I shouldn't have to tell you of all people how much the club depends on advance season ticket sales to see it through the long summer months.'

'Yes, Chair,' Jack replied humbly, not knowing what there was to add.

'How many had we sold this time last year?'

That was the one question he had hoped he wouldn't be asked! Did he tell the truth, or say he had to check the figures? It might buy him some time but he didn't want to appear even more clueless. He decided to come out with the uncomfortable truth: 'About 3500, Chair.'

'That's not good! Not good at all!' The Chair looked shaken to the core. He just sat there, frozen.

As an instinct of pure self-defence Jack averted his eyes, looking at anything but the man sitting opposite him. It felt uncomfortable, as though waiting for Arnold Preston to explode or whatever. No, Jack reminded himself, one could bank on Arnold keeping calm in adversity. Even so, iron control could sometimes be more frightening in its effect than if he threw the odd wobbler. Perhaps it was the politician in him that dictated he keep dignified in all circumstances.

Arnold folded his arms tightly across his chest, in self-discipline. The tension, waiting for him to say something, was almost unbearable. Then he finally let out with: 'Does the auditing firm know about this?'

'No, I only got the updated figures this morning, Chair.'

'But you must have had some idea things weren't going well?'

Jack squirmed. He wanted to say it wasn't his fault but didn't think saying so would go down well at that moment. Besides, he knew the Chair would be astute enough to work it out for himself. He kept silent.

'Does Simon know about this?'

'The manager is on holiday,' Jack answered diplomatically.

'Of course . . . of course.'

'I could contact him if you like.'

'No, the young man's entitled to his break.'

Jack knew how protective the Chair always was of the manager. An alternative sprang into his mind. 'I could get in touch with the new man?'

'That's not a bad idea!' The Chair seemed positively enthused. 'He's not on holiday as well, is he though?'

'I know he's around because he's taken up the keys to that house of ours on the estate.'

'Yes do that, Jack. Reminds me, I'm preparing something to present to the players for the start of the season. Think they'll need an explanation from me about the respective roles of the two managers.'

Jack nodded acquiescently. At least this exchange between them hadn't been as unsettling to his nervous system as the one a few days ago.

'Is that it, Chair?'

'Yes, for the time being at least.'

'Very well, Chair.'

'Make sure you get in touch with Borrow though. That side

of things could well become part of his brief. Simon has enough on dealing with the playing side.'

Reflecting on matters, after the Chair had left him in peace again, Jack saw the main thing was that he had succeeded in extricating himself from any possible blame. But as far as Simon's part was concerned, he hadn't cared to tell the Chair his blue-eyed boy had been boasting for weeks that he was going to make sure, through his own personal efforts, that season tickets for 10/11 sold like hot cakes.

Putting all that aside, one good thing about having the 'new man' on board was that he was surely experienced enough to be able to suggest the right course of action. So long as he didn't poke his nose too much into other people's business, things might even improve this season. Certainly, they couldn't possibly get worse.

It is the interval during a performance of Madame Butterfly at The Lowry Theatre in Manchester. Her companion Martin is avidly reading the programme. At least, in the style of the true gentleman he is, he has made sure of pre-ordering a glass of wine each for them so that they didn't have to get involved in any unseemly scramble at the bar. Emily is being careful she doesn't have too much to drink though, because they've already been out for dinner with a champagne starter and then shared a bottle of sauvignon blanc.

As a museum curator, Martin has broad cultural tastes. 'Eclectic' is probably the word he would use. This is the third time during the last three months they have gone out together for dinner followed by an arts event. They have been to see a play, a ballet and now tonight an opera. Emily can't help picking out that Martin is very keen on all the historical background. For example he likes to talk at length about the factors that influenced the playwright or the choreographer, or now the librettist, to create their particular piece of work. Later tonight, possibly if they choose to have a coffee afterwards, Martin will no doubt present a cogently argued thesis on how Puccini based his work on actual examples of Japanese girls fatally believing in the rash promises of foreigners. That is her hunch as to how the evening will finish. Meanwhile, what compels her own interest, although she cannot find it in her heart to admit it to Martin, is the sheer passion behind the storyline and its powerful rendition in sound and enthralling emotion.

Over recent months the relationship has at least served to add a much-needed extra dimension to her social life. Coming back to live in the north-west was not what she had ever expected. Nor would she have guessed, as little as twelve months ago, that she would end up feeling so lonely and drawn in on herself. Emily still couldn't decide whether it was a sign of renewed hopeful-ness or just plain desperation that had led her to place an advert on a soulmate website. It had been hard at first overcoming qualms about somehow putting herself 'on the market'. This was followed by all the agonising over how she would present herself in her profile. Reconciling herself to the fact there were inevitably in-built difficulties in the whole nature of the exercise, not least the limited number of words available to do justice to the pen-portrait, she had just about managed to satisfy herself it was a process worth submitting to. If she had to give any special emphasis to what she was looking for in a 'soulmate' it would be someone who was good company going out to dinner with before going on to a cultural event.

Enter dear Martin! In terms of matching the specifications, he might have appeared to be the complete Mr Right. But that was the trouble. However much of a gentleman he was, she knew it was never fated to go beyond their pleasant social occasions together. To be fair to Martin, he didn't himself seem to hold out any unreal expectations beyond meeting up socially. Besides, he seemed much too interested in pursuing academic matters.

While in some respects it filled a gap for her, Emily still felt residually troubled by the recent adverse turn of events in her life. Chief among her concerns, she had not found it easy returning to the town where she grew up. It was like an admission of defeat. She was the sister who had gone away to university and whose horizons had at one time seemed boundless.

By contrast, her younger sister Laura had always seemed to keep to the steady ground. She had stayed on into the sixth form but then had been more than happy to find a job locally. She had met Mark through work. They had got married in their mid-20s and now had two children, Tom 14 and Samantha 12. Laura was the one who had always been around for their mum, especially during the last five widowed years after the death of their father.

Although more than aware of the important stages and time-lines in the lives of other members of her immediate family, Emily had at the same time become increasingly depressed about the fact that her 40th birthday was looming up on her in two months' time in August. If she had felt fulfilled in either her work or her life, this apprehension might not have been so acute.

What made the present situation even harder to bear was that, until two years ago, everything she had dreamed of achieving had still seemed possible. Then, within the space of a twelve-month period, her prestigious job in the business world had folded, followed by the end of her long-term relationship with Edward when he had walked out on her to live with another woman. After that, she no longer wanted or even could afford to go on living in London. Desperate to retain some semblance of stability in her life, she seemed to have had little realistic choice but to return to the north-west and take a job as a temp in the meantime.

Her job at the football club had proved the most interesting work she had taken on so far. Even though she didn't know how long it would last, she was glad it was now being extended. Before the end of the year she also had her holiday in Italy to look forward to. This was to be a kind of belated birthday treat. The tour included places like Florence and Lucca, the birthplace of the composer of Madame Butterfly. She would also be visiting

Siena, which was another reason why she had been interested to see that Frank Borrow had once managed the football club there. He might at least be able to recommend a restaurant to go to while she was there.

6

'I'm sorry if my next question sounds a bit personal but . . .'

The reporter hesitated for a moment, almost inviting a response. Hunching his shoulders, Frank felt the question coming on regardless. It had been a fairly harmless interview so far by normal standards, but he knew the way reporters always saved up the last question to cut to the quick.

'Why, Frank, at your age, do you still feel the need to stay in football management?'

The question sounded even more pointed for the fact that the reporter was probably only in his mid 20s. It was preferable of course not to let it look like he was taking it personally. Best also not to appear to be thinking too carefully about the answer because it would only betray insecurity.

'Because I still remain enthusiastic about my job!' he rapped out, matter-of-factly.

'Yes . . . yes.' The reporter jotted down the response in his pad, appearing satisfied on the face of it. Only he was obviously pursuing a theme: 'Of course there are quite a few of you managers around . . . Er, no offence intended! For example there's Wenger, Redknapp, not to mention Sir Alex himself.'

Momentarily flattered to hear himself included in such an impressive roll-call, something left Frank waiting for a sting in the tail.

'Giants in the game go on enjoying success season after season.' A telling pause again. 'What would you say to the idea it's all a bit addictive . . . even something of an aphrodisiac?'

43

For them, possibly. For himself, he hadn't noticed it! He merely gave a non-committal smile back. That only seemed to draw the sting.

'Do you feel the same sensation going to . . . Oakhill United Football Club?'

Suddenly, the nightmare memory of the DVD played vividly back into his mind. All the managerial names the reporter had mentioned were riding high and, if anything, scaling new peaks. It couldn't help troubling him that he'd hit rock bottom.

However, another crisply delivered answer was called for. 'My aim has always been to do my very best by every club I've served at. As I said, I'm really looking forward to starting the new season at Oakhill United. Now if you don't mind.' Frank felt like winding things up at this stage. He'd given the reporter half an hour already.

'One last question, Mr Borrow, if you don't mind?'

Despite glancing meaningfully at his watch, Frank conceded. 'Well, OK, one last question.'

'How do you think it'll work having two managers at Oakhill United?'

All his experience told him that reporters, even young ones, were not daft. Unscrupulous, perhaps, but not daft. But he wasn't biting on that bait. He answered simply: 'I'm sure it's going to work out very well.'

Not to be thwarted so easily, the reporter was angling for a supplementary. But Frank wasn't up for it. 'Thank you, it's been a pleasure. The PA will show you out.'

'Thank you for your time, Frank,' the reporter politely finished. 'Can I come back for a follow-up interview at some point?'

Before Frank had time to answer, the other man had followed up with, 'If you don't mind me saying, good luck for the season ahead.'

Frank didn't react. After all, running the gauntlet of reporters, like getting sacked, was just another occupational hazard.

*   *   *

'Flaming reporters!'

Emily was at first a bit taken aback to hear Frank Borrow sounding off. Then a twinkle in his eye told her it was just for show and that he wasn't really angry. But still she thought she'd better make allowance. It would be misguided of her to take anything for granted at this stage.

'Do you want me just to say no in future? I could do . . . if you like?' she said, wanting to be helpful.

'Hmm, it never gets any easier. It's an essential part of their job description to be slightly vile and obnoxious. Sometimes not just slightly!'

A bit strong, she thought. But again there was something in his tone that said he could handle it. And she couldn't miss his sense of humour. At least, it suggested her awkward handling of the transfer of the house keys hadn't rebounded on her entirely.

'Going on about my age! Is it a fair matter to raise?'

Interpreting this as a rhetorical question, she didn't say anything, expecting him to go on. He didn't though. Instead he actually seemed to be asking her what she thought. Taken by surprise, she just smiled. Thankfully she must have passed the test because he merely returned the smile.

As he hovered by her desk still, a slight nervousness made her blurt out the first thing that came into her head. 'Are you settling in OK at the new house?' As soon as the words had escaped her lips, she thought what a stupid thing to say. For it would only remind him of the way she had abandoned him high and dry that day.

'Yes,' he replied thoughtfully. 'You saw it yourself. It's no mansion, is it? But I suppose it'll do for the moment.'

She sensed it wasn't a topic he wanted to discuss much further. But as he kept standing there, and she looked between him and her work, she didn't know what else to say. It even crossed her mind to try and lead into asking him about good restaurants in Siena but it definitely wouldn't have been the right moment for that.

'Until I find somewhere else, that is,' he said filling up the space. 'By the way, is Jack around, do you know?'

Yes, safer to get back to business. Feeling more comfortable, she replied efficiently, 'Yes, he's seeing the secretary of the Supporters' Club in his office right now.'

'Only I need to see him about a message he's left me about the amount of advance pre-season ticket sales.' A slight pause. 'Or rather, should I say, the lack of.'

Again something in his turn of phrase couldn't help but amuse her. But she also remembered half-catching the end of some conversation between Jack and the Chair about a 'real crisis' and that 'the new man would be best dealing with it'. Perhaps she shouldn't risk taking Frank Borrow's slightly jokey approach too much at face value. Until she got to know his ways a little better there was a risk, she warned herself, of misreading something into his manner that might not actually be there. Oh god, was she over-complicating things again?

'Well he should be free by about 10.30, I think,' she responded in businesslike mode.

'I'll try and see him then. If you can let him know, I would be grateful. By the way, any chance of another coffee?'

'I'll go and make you one straight away.' Standing over the kettle in the kitchen, she reflected on their conversation. For all that it had been fairly mundane in terms of content, there was always something about his manner which kept her guessing.

Emily had been hoping to have something worthwhile to take round to Laura's for her nephew Tom. Perhaps a football signed by the whole Oakhill United team. But because it was the close season and very few of the players were around, this was something which would have to wait. Knowing her luck, her extended time at the club would run out at exactly the time the new season was swinging into full motion.

'So what's the most interesting part about working at the football club?' Tom had wanted to know in that precocious, grounded way of his. According to Laura he had just had his first careers lesson at school. The teachers had been preparing pupils to think carefully about what they wanted to do for their work experience opportunity in twelve months' time.

'Well it's hard to say because the old season has ended and the new season hasn't started.' Emily realised it was hardly the most compelling of answers to a 14-year-old with a low boredom threshold.

'You mean nothing interesting is happening at all,' Tom concluded fairly dismissively.

'I wouldn't say that.'

'Doesn't sound very thrilling to me . . .'

Wracking her brain to think of something original, the best she could come up with was: 'A new Executive Manager has just been appointed, Frank Borrow.' She tried to give the name special emphasis as if it was someone he was bound to have heard of.

But to her dismay he only stared back blankly at her. 'Who?'

'I've heard of Frank Borrow!' Tom's dad piped up from nowhere. Emily hadn't noticed that Mark had just slipped through the front door, home from work. 'The Professor! Or should I say *Il Professore*? He had a spell as a manager in Italy if my memory serves me right.'

Since it was obvious the name of Frank Borrow struck a chord with his dad, Tom couldn't help looking impressed himself.

'Is there any chance of you sorting me a work experience placement at the club?' Tom suddenly asked.

'Don't pester, Tom! I'm sure Aunt Emily will do her best nearer the time.'

Emily might have been over-reacting but although she was normally quite lukewarm to her rather dour brother-in-law, at that moment she felt extraordinarily like giving him a hug.

Despite all the rather worrying signs that seemed to be emerging at Oakhill United, Frank knew that he always relished a challenge. The tougher the better! While accepting that the job of a football manager was stressful, staying in there was very much an adrenaline factor. If anyone had assumed he had been ready to quit his career a month ago, he had proved them wrong. Not that he didn't realise the day would come sometime. But all he knew was that he wasn't ready for it yet. For the moment, it simply didn't feel right.

For one thing, there was his pride. He still wanted to finish on a high. However much he was able to concentrate on a future at Oakhill United, hardly a night passed when some memory or other of the last few strained weeks in his previous management role didn't simmer to the surface of his mind with disturbing effect. But how would he cope if he didn't have football to occupy his life? His thoughts veered back to the reporter and his reference to the breed of 60-plus managers who seemingly couldn't let go. Then he thought of famous managers in the past, many of whom had arguably retired too early, like Bill Shankly at Liverpool, and the hole it had created in their lives that they had never somehow been able to fill. And it wasn't as if Shankly hadn't had a strong family life to support him through the wilderness years that followed on from his glory trail at Anfield. Retiring too soon had literally ripped the man's heart out.

Not that Frank had family to enjoy or even fall back on. That was another telling spin-off from his journey to Siena. It had constituted a final severing of all that life in Italy could have provided him with. Apart from the potential it had offered in footballing terms, he had once held out hope of starting a family with his young Italian bride after the breakdown of his marriage to Penny. It was perhaps another element to the thinly disguised contempt that Carla's family had come to feel for him that he had not stayed in Tuscany to rear *bambini*. If things had turned out right for him in the job, no doubt he would have dearly wished for the same himself. But, as he had irrevocably to accept, the end had now been reached.

This particular afternoon, although handyman work around the house wasn't the strongest of his attributes, he had decided to take a hammer and nails to hang the mementoes of his championship-winning teams on the walls of his new abode, one framed picture per storey. How dearly though, he was thinking, he would also have liked keepsake evidence somewhere on a ledge or bookcase of living family.

Both his parents were dead and he had no brothers or sisters, nor did he have children from either of his marriages. Now, to all intents and purposes, he was divorced. But just as in footballing terms he had never been a quitter and had always looked for a new challenge, there was still something in his psyche that would not give way and admit defeat. In the same way that taking on his role at Oakhill United looked anything but a bed of roses in prospect, so he had to go on taking responsibility for his life and not resign himself to lack of fulfilment and the torment self-abandonment might cost him in years to come.

Preoccupied with such thoughts, something at the back of his mind told him he had heard a knock on his front door. Oh dear, not that boy Ben again, was his first reaction. But glancing out of his first floor window, thankfully he could see no sign of anyone at the door. Almost in a panic instinct, not to say a desire to avert the prospect of the lad turning up unexpectedly again in the meantime, he had decided the best thing he could do was to return the DVD straight away with a note of thanks through the letterbox of 3 Queen Anne's Way. After all, putting on some trainers, he had only to nip a few metres down the road. In one decisive act he could curtail the chance of any possible follow-up visit.

Approaching the house in question, he darted a stealthy glance up at the first floor window, knowing that was where anyone was likely to be looking out from. The red sports car was absent from the drive, and he calculated it another good sign. Tiptoeing the last few steps to the front door, he quietly released the DVD case through the letterbox and turned on his heel.

Barely a second after dispatching the cargo his nerves were shattered by the door instantly shooting open, as though on a coiled spring. He was greeted by the figure of Rosie Skipton, dressed in a rather dilapidated-looking pair of overalls.

'Why if it isn't Mr Executive Manager . . . sir!' she exclaimed in what came across as an exaggeratedly respectful tone of voice. 'Look at me though! Trust you to catch me doing housework.'

Frank stood there like a naughty boy caught scrumping apples.

'Well I always finish with dusting down the front door. Are you coming in or not? I'll just go and get changed while I put the kettle on. Why it's lovely to see you again!'

Perhaps it was down to discomfiture and sense of guilt but there seemed no way he could refuse the offer.

7

Frank couldn't deny feeling a strange sense of unease entering Rosie Skipton's house. It was embarrassing enough that he had been caught red-handed trying to sneak the DVD back through the letterbox and running. How ill-considered in retrospect did that seem as a tactic? It had backfired to the extent that he had instead put himself at the complete mercy of having to accept her offer of hospitality. Perhaps, if he had had his wits about him, he could still have mustered up a polite refusal. But now he had willingly acceded to her request, it was too late.

Glancing up and down the road to satisfy himself no-one was watching him as he crossed the threshold, he tried hard to keep reassuring himself he was behaving in the way a decent, sociable neighbour would. Once inside, he shouldn't really have been surprised to find the house had exactly the same three-storey dimensions as his own. Rosie motioned him up the stairs to the lounge on the first floor.

Rather late in the day, he was now ashamedly wondering whether she was married or not. Why would he do that? For some reason, he reckoned she wasn't. Yes, she wore a ring on the appropriate finger, except it hadn't looked imposing enough to be a wedding ring. But why, he berated himself, should it make a scrap of difference to him whether there was any other man in her life?

'If you don't mind. I'll just go and get changed into something a bit more in the style of a lady offering tea to a gentleman,' she said to him in a way that suggested she might return in a kimono or some such outfit. Or was that just his imagination running away with him?

Since she hadn't actually asked him to sit down, he hovered in front of a settee not wanting to look presumptuous. Meanwhile, he couldn't help catching sight on surface-tops of pictures of Ben, herself and family and friends.

'Sit down, please do. Make yourself comfortable,' she offered brightly on re-appearing. Before he could say anything, she continued, 'By the way, I rather think you were hiding your light under a bushel last time we met. You didn't let on you were the new Executive Manager of Oakhill United Football Club, did you?' Her manner of speaking had a teasing edge to it which slightly conveyed a posh girl's public school accent. Although he couldn't quite tell whether it was affected, or else her natural style of utterance, he certainly couldn't imagine her having been brought up in this part of town.

His self-protective instinct was to say he would have been all too ready to tell her on that previous occasion, just that she hadn't really let him get a word in edgeways. A bit like now, he thought, but best to keep this to himself this time too!

As if reading his mind, she exclaimed: 'I'm not gushing again, am I? It's nerves, you know. All my friends say I have a habit of babbling on too much.' She let out the same self-conscious giggle that he recalled from their last encounter and he felt a similar emotion of warmth towards her.

But he still somehow didn't risk venturing a response. What was it about being in her company that rendered him so tongue-tied? Instead he found himself noticing how elegantly she was attired in a crisp, white shirt and smart designer jeans, which served to accentuate her slim figure.

'Yes and I'm very grateful to Ben for having given me the chance to view the DVD,' he said, trying to win back some Brownie points he might have lost along the way. Finally giving vent to his vocal cords might also prevent her writing him off for having the conversational skills of a Trappist monk.

'By the way, you've just missed Ben.'

'Pardon?' he offered back feebly. How could he put it in a diplomatic way that he hadn't been trying to see Ben? In fact the very opposite.

'He should be back in half an hour's time though.' Rosie seemed set on reassuring him.

'I'm not sure if I can stay that long,' he said, beginning to feel a fresh sense of unease.

'I'm so proud of Ben,' she interjected. 'You know he's had to go through so much in his life so far.'

Sensing from the sudden fervour in her voice that she was intent on enlarging on the sheer scope of difficulties her son had had to endure, he felt it appropriate just to nod again in sympathy as she continued, 'Ben's father left him when he was ten . . . it was very, very difficult. Especially since his father hasn't ever paid a penny yet in alimony or support.'

Apart from the content of what she was saying, her habit of leaving charged pauses between short snatches of sentences was quite disconcerting. He wasn't sure whether she was merely pausing to check his reaction or whether he was supposed to offer something in response. He decided the earnestness of the look on her face meant she was on a flow and that she preferred the licence just to press on with her tale.

'Ben never had an easy time at school . . . he was always being targeted . . . not just by pupils but by teachers . . . many times I had to go into school to sort out difficulties . . . Ben was always seen as different . . . he's always suffered by somehow being seen as different.'

There was plenty in what she was saying that he might have felt like unpicking a bit more. But Rosie articulated herself with such strong, emotional engagement and with such compelling conviction on her son's behalf that it would have seemed churlish, not to say almost a sacrilege, to try and halt her in mid-stride.

'By the way, I seem to remember offering you some tea?' she suddenly broke off. A wide rainbow-effect smile broke through.

'I rather think you did,' he said 'but if . . .'

'How awful of me to forget! What a poor hostess! Getting carried away about Ben . . . would you care to join me in the kitchen and we can go on talking?' she said with the natural expectation that he would follow her.

'Football is Ben's real passion . . . he's really good at it! Andy, the Academy manager, thought the world of Ben . . . it was such a pity when Andy left . . . the new manager, I think I told you, dropped Ben . . . Ben was heart-broken . . . he really seems to have gone off the rails since then . . . his school work has suffered as a result . . . Do you take milk in your tea . . . sugar?'

All the time she was talking, Frank distractedly watched her as she put teabags into the cups, poured the water out of the kettle and slipped milk into the cups. But what commanded his attention above all, he couldn't deny, was the figure she cut in her jeans and the arresting way she had, which had taken him by surprise more than once, of turning round to stare at him with an expression of great intensity. Besides that, there didn't seem any real imperative for him to take an active part. The most productive role it seemed he could play was as a good listener. As such, he couldn't really go wrong . . . and the more willing he was to listen and be understanding, the more appreciative she seemed to be of his company.

Fortunately when the time came for Frank to go, Ben had not yet arrived back. As she opened the door, she thanked him for returning the DVD. It was kind of her to do so. He took it upon himself to comment on the fact that her red sports car was nowhere to be seen.

'Yes, I had terrible trouble arranging the insurance for the dented wing. The repair company it's in with now says I won't be able to get it back until the end of the week. It's a terrible business as I have such a long way to travel to work and the bus service is very slow and unreliable.'

Listening to her transport plight, he only narrowly resisted an instinct, there and then, to offer to ferry her into work himself in the meantime. Some thin remaining vestige of reserve kicked in just in time to save him from the risk of sounding much too forward on the flimsy pretext of two brief meetings. At the door, he thanked her again for the tea.

'You will promise to do your best by Ben, won't you?' she said entreatingly. 'Even if it's only having a chat about football in general. He really would appreciate that. And so would I!'

'Of course, I will,' he responded, basking in the radiance of the smile she bestowed upon him.

'Been trying to get hold of you all day!' It was Jack Hubbard's voice sounding flustered on the other end of the line.

'Yes?' Frank answered.

'Normally I'd raise this one with Simon. But as you know he's still on his break. The Chair said I should let you know in the meantime. Only, we've just found out three of our players have been snapped up this week on close season transfers! Free transfers of course but the beggars have been enticed by better offers of personal terms by other clubs.'

'Isn't there anything at all we can do at this stage?' Frank asked hopefully.

'No, sounds like they've signed on the dotted line.'

'Who are the players in question?'

'Brown, Marrison and Pierce. If the names mean anything to you. That is, you being new to the club,' Jack quickly corrected himself.

But having seen the DVD, the names did mean something to Frank. In fact, they were the only players he reckoned had come out of the game with any credit at all. Perhaps, although he didn't like to say it to Jack, the main reason why they were leaving was because they saw the writing on the wall.

'The only consolation is that I know Simon didn't particularly rate them,' Jack went on. 'The three of them had only joined the club at the start of last season on one-year contracts. Fly-by-nights if you ask me! Not the type of players we're used to at

Oakhill United that the Chair would call loyal to the club.'

'Well, I suppose if they were only on one-year contracts, it was a bit predictable, wasn't it?' Frank said, a little more flippantly than he had intended. 'Do you know if it had been considered whether to renew their contracts?'

'You'd have to ask the gaffer that,' came back the non-committal but predictable reply. 'All I know is it leaves us with a bit of a gap as far as experienced players are concerned. Not the best place to be in with the start of the new season looming. Just thought I'd let you know.'

'When did you say Simon gets back?'

'This coming Monday.'

Yes, Frank should have remembered. It was this coming Tuesday, in only four days' time, when the Chair had arranged the meeting to introduce him to the players and inform them about how he and Simon would be working together.

'Not a lot we can do, I suppose, until Simon gets back,' Jack ventured by way of a conclusion to the conversation.

'Thanks, Jack.'

The main afterthought that occurred to Frank at the end of the phone call was that if he had been manager in his own right, he would be spending every hour between now and next Tuesday doing his level best to attract players from other clubs to join Oakhill United. But he didn't suppose he could really. Not just on his own initiative, that was. The best it seemed he could do in the meantime was to scout around unofficially, see what he could come up with and then have a conversation with Simon Steele as early as possible next week. Then hopefully the two of them might be able to see eye-to-eye about what needed doing next.

The text on Rosie Skipton's mobile read:

> *Going out with mates. Stopping at dad's tonight.*

Thank goodness, then, she hadn't tried to keep Frank Borrow there until Ben had got back. He would have had to stay until the next day at least! It was annoying though that Ben was yet again using his dad, and that dreadful woman he lived with, as a convenient port of call. Not that her dear ex-hubby would be bound to be in himself. He and his woman would gad off somewhere and just leave Ben the key. The last time she'd done that herself, Ben had invited all and sundry and she'd come home to find the place trashed. Galling to admit, she knew Ben wouldn't dream of doing that to his dad's home. It wasn't respect or anything. Just that he knew his father would kick him out and never have him back again. The cheek of it was that, according to Ben, the stupid woman was always banging on about how spoilt rotten he'd been by his mother and how much he needed more discipline. Well what would that bitch know?

Anyway, she didn't think she was too soft on him by any means. Not that it was exactly the same for her. Even if she did rather look after Ben, serving him his favourite meals night and day, it would have been a severe blow to her pride if he didn't treat her house as his home.

Something in her felt like irritating Ben a bit. Taking up her mobile, she texted back:

> *Pity u were out! Frank Borrow – u know new Exec Manager – called round. See u tomorrow. Take care x*

A matter of only seconds later, her mobile bleeped frantically:

> *What? Why didn't u call me? What he come for?*

It felt unusual and strangely satisfying to have her son so desperate to be in contact with her. She experienced pleasure in seeking to wind him up even more:

Oakhill Utd short of players at moment and he wondered if u could come round for trial for first team tomorrow?

Perhaps she had pitched it a bit over the top this time because his next message just said:

LOL mum

A couple of minutes later though, he'd obviously given it more thought and there was another bleep:

Seriously whats he want?

How should she respond? Just tell the truth, she decided. She tapped in the words *Just returned DVD* but then thought better of it, deleted the message and tapped in the following instead:

To see u say thank u for your kindness lending him DVD.

And then almost as soon as she'd put her mobile down again, the quick reply came:

Great mum. Hope u were nice to him?

Oh yes, she thought, she had been nice as pie! For one thing, she supposed she could have made him feel much more uncomfortable about trying to drop the DVD back without anyone knowing. She certainly needn't have invited him in for tea. For a moment, particularly when he'd seen her appearance, she didn't think he looked in favour of staying at all. But it was amazing how much more relaxed he seemed to become after she'd slipped into something else and come back down to talk to him. She only hoped she hadn't put him off with her habit of nattering on too much. No, somehow, she didn't think so.

On reflection, there was definitely something about the way he had seemed to react that made her feel confident she couldn't have made that bad an impression on him. Call it a woman's intuition.

8

In Frank's experience, players' changing rooms were rowdy hell-holes. Anyone in so-called authority had to learn the hard way about the art of imposing themselves in there.

Today though, it certainly had to be the first time Frank had ever entered changing rooms to find every single player sitting motionless under their pegs with eyes turned down to the floor. Not a whisper! It felt more as if he had wandered by mistake into a prayer room.

True, it was the first day of a new season. Added to that, it was probably very unusual for the Chairman of the Board himself to have called a meeting for the players. They could no doubt be excused for thinking there was some out-of-the-ordinary reason for it.

Besides, most of them had been away for at least a week or two and needed a bit of time to reacclimatise to work. There again, the subdued air might be simply out of politeness and respect to the Chair. Trying hard to see it from the players' point of view, Frank thought it must have seemed heavy duty for them to have all three figures striding into their territory – Chair, Simon Steele and himself.

If the odd player's eye flickered up in the direction of today's welcoming committee, Frank had soon become uncomfortably aware that most eyes focused on himself rather than the other two. Not so surprising, he supposed, bearing in mind Arnold Preston and Simon Steele were familiar figures to the players. As he sensed very well, it was he who would be seen as the unknown quantity. If he hadn't fully appreciated it before, Frank realised now the crucial importance of how his role was going to be perceived, especially by the players.

The Chair, looking every inch his usual calm and collected self, seemed mindful of allowing a few seconds to pass before choosing the right moment to address the players. Meanwhile, standing next to Simon Steele, Frank observed the scowl on the other man's face as he shifted his weight uneasily from one foot to the other while impatiently waiting for the Chair to take it upon himself to proceed.

'Welcome back, gentlemen,' the Chair started with a smooth almost deliberately casual-sounding style that seemed intent on defusing any strained atmosphere. 'I hope you've had a restful week or two and are now in the mood to give your all once again for Oakhill United in the coming season.'

One or two of the more senior players seemed visibly to become more relaxed and look up. Slowly, the younger players followed suit, beginning to lift their eyes from the floor. At least they weren't getting a bollocking for the poor form of last season!

'It is my other duty though,' the Chair continued, 'to tell you that we're looking to make changes in how the club is managed this season.'

As the Chair paused, a slight tension re-asserted itself on the brows of the players. Nor could Frank help but notice how Simon Steele reacted to the start of this statement by folding his arms stiffly across his chest.

'Well perhaps not so much making a change, rather providing more support and, er, capacity . . .'

At the word 'capacity', Frank detected one or two uncertain exchanges of glances between players.

'The Board continues to have every confidence in the work that Simon Steele has done in the very short time since he was appointed to the post of manager at the club. But certain extra pressures on the club make it advisable for the Board to look to make an additional appointment, for the short term at least, of a manager with a great amount of experience for us to make use of as well . . .'

Seeming to begin to warm to his explanation, the Chair at this point suddenly wheeled round, with the air of a magician waving a wand, to Frank standing a pace or two behind, and announced, 'Here then is Frank Borrow, who is joining Oakhill in support of Simon as the manager.'

With the cat now decidedly out of the bag, Frank became the burning object of attention for a few sustained seconds as all eyes focused on him with a fierce intensity. Perhaps just to show he was human like the rest of them, he felt an impulse to say something to try and put them at their ease a bit more.

However, as he was about to start, the Chair stepped in again. 'By the way, does anyone have any questions they would like to put? To me, that is, in the first instance.'

Slightly nonplussed, Frank was only aware of the players exchanging more knowing glances. Then suddenly one of the players spoke up forthrightly. 'Is all this happening, Chair, because there's a danger of Oakhill going into administration?'

'Into administration?' Repeating the words but trying to impart some almost light-hearted element, the Chair went on to answer the question seriously with what Frank could see was the consummate art of the politician.

'Jed, Oakhill United has always been a solvent club, properly managed by the Board, and I can assure you all, while I'm still Chair of the club it always will be in future!'

Jed, who Frank remembered from the DVD as a journeyman full-back with a disturbing lack of pace, sat back more easily in response to this answer.

'Only there's a rumour going round that season ticket sales have bombed and there's no money for new players to replace those that have gone,' piped up another voice.

Frank felt almost a touch of relief that the first few questions, serious as they were, seemed to be centring on other issues than himself.

'I can assure you too, John,' the Chair again took it upon himself to reply, 'the Board places greatest importance of all on what takes place out there on the football field. Wherever we think we need to boost our squad, we will endeavour to do so.'

But John didn't seem so satisfied and raised his hand to ask another question: 'What's the point in having two managers?'

Noticeably, other players sat up as if keen too to know the real thinking behind the move.

'I thought I'd explained,' said the Chair with a touch of impatience in his voice. 'As I said, Simon is the manager and Frank will work alongside him to share the load for a year in the first instance. Simon remains the manager and Frank, in an executive manager role, will work in partnership with him.'

As the Chair was speaking, Frank could feel players' eyes switching uncomfortably between himself and Simon.

'Is that all, then?' said the Chair, very much appearing to want to wrap up proceedings at this point. 'Well, can I wish you a good season ahead? Don't forget, the Board will give you our full support!'

Apart from one or two token nods back from players, it was noticeable to Frank that, by the end of the meeting, there still were far more questions in players' minds than answers.

'Back here at 10.30 for a team talk, followed by training and five-a-side up to lunch,' boomed out the voice of Simon Steele.

Certainly the players looked happier to be told they were getting down to business.

'If that's all right with you, that is?' Simon turned around a moment or two later to address Frank privately.

Somehow appreciative of Simon talking to him at all, Frank said cooperatively, 'That's fine.'

Together the three of them wandered back to Simon's office.

'I think that went well,' pronounced the Chair. 'The players will soon get used to the new arrangements.'

'Matt Johnson was looking for you.'

Catching a quizzical look on Frank's face, Emily thought she had better give more information: 'Matt's the Head of Oakhill United Academy.'

'Do you know what it's about?' Frank asked.

'I think he was just wanting to say hello and introduce himself,' Emily replied.

Matt had asked Emily where Frank's office was going to be, but she had to admit she didn't know what the arrangements were yet.

'I'm out and about the place today, so no doubt I'll bump into him sometime.' Frank left it at that.

Emily had been curious to see how Frank would approach his first official day at work. She had wondered whether he would don an Oakhill United tracksuit with the letters FB across his chest. If so, she hoped he would manage to lay his hands on a better-fitting one than Simon Steele's! But in the event he'd arrived in suit and tie, a different one from that which he had worn at interview but in a similar classic Italian style. She noticed he had joined Simon for the team talk and appeared to have stayed for a lot of the morning session.

Perhaps she should make a more direct point of asking him where he was going to make his office? But not knowing how much longer she might be asked to stay on at the club, she didn't like to make any assumptions about her own right to ask or say things. During the close season weeks she had merely done what anyone such as the Chair or Jack Hubbard had required her to do. But now Simon Steele and Frank Borrow were both on site full time, it naturally raised questions in her mind as to how her role would operate in these new circumstances. But then she supposed everyone at Oakhill must be having similar such thoughts on Day One.

Frank had hoped he wouldn't feel too much like a fish out of water on his first day at work, but it was beginning to feel awfully like that. When Emily mentioned that someone was looking for him, if it had been a normal situation he had been coming into, he would merely have told her to arrange a time for the person to come and see him in his office.

Of course, he accepted he had to take a fair bit of responsibility for the fact that he hadn't got himself sorted out for the start of the new season. He should really have taken better advantage of the one or two days when he had visited the club during the close season, for example, organising basic things like finding office space for himself.

Somehow that aspect hadn't seemed quite so important then in the general scheme of things. And in any case he would have needed to confer with Simon Steele who, at the time, had been away on holiday. Frank had even held out the optimistic hope that when Simon returned he would suggest Frank share his office. He would have thought that would be a good idea for them because it would have shown from the start that they were a team and intent on working together.

But when Frank had tentatively suggested such a possibility first thing this morning, the look on Simon's face had been a picture. It was clearly a case of 'over his dead body'. The stubborn refusal to enter into any related discussion conveyed the absolute impression that, as they say, possession is nine-tenths of the law! And Simon would be of a mind to keep it that way as long as he possibly could. Frank would only have shared if Simon had been willing. But Simon had made it his personal den, with the walls plastered over with all those tired management clichés like 'The Buck Stops Here!' and 'When the Going Gets Tough, The Tough Get Going!'

In these circumstances, Frank had to ask himself did he want to, or even need to, make a point by 'taking over' or trying to force Simon to share his office with him? No, he had instinctively decided against any such approach. For despite the fact that Simon's manner could never be described as welcoming, Frank had set himself against any tone which could be seen as confrontational. Until he had any stronger evidence to go on, he felt determined to keep it that way.

Besides, Frank had tried to see things a bit more from the players' point of view earlier that morning, and he felt he also needed to empathise with how Simon must be feeling. While pride was obviously kicking in big-time with the young man, Frank could quite easily see where it was all coming from. As he knew very well himself from looking back on his own first appointment to the post of manager so many years ago, the act of moving into the manager's office and seeing your name on the door represented a massive sense of achievement. To then have to see someone else's name appearing alongside yours, let alone the possibility of it appearing above your name – especially with an elevated-sounding title like Executive Manager – couldn't help but present a grim prospect to Simon.

However, thinking considerately didn't sort out where Frank was actually going. In the meantime he would have to find some temporary space at least. Otherwise, anyone wanting to see him could be excused for thinking he was a nomad on the run. He was determined to have a chat with Emily and see what could be arranged.

Emily had exercised her initiative by contacting the site supervisor. He in turn had not taken too kindly to having to find somewhere to put the new man. According to how Emily relayed it to him later, it sounded as if he had been expecting Frank to arrive with his own portakabin.

While hardly comforted by the gist of what she was saying, he was quietly amused by Emily's style of reporting back to him. There was something pleasantly conspiratorial about her manner. It was as if to say that however inefficient everything was at this place, the two of them could do worse than share a philosophical approach in the face of current frustrations.

At the end of Emily's deliberations with the site supervisor, it had transpired that, unless Frank wished to take it upon himself to turf someone out of their existing office, he had to make a dubious choice from two possibilities. One was a small area the

size of a broom cupboard that hadn't been used since being abandoned by someone who'd been at the club on a short-term govern-
ment training scheme. The second was the club's interview room
which was presently used on an 'ad hoc' booking system for meetings as and when required. Of the two, mindful that the arrangement was hopefully only temporary, he opted for the second
alternative. Not without reservations, because the problem with
the interview room was that although it was comparatively
spacious, it was positioned in the front entrance area and as open
to view as a goldfish bowl.

'By the way, someone else has been trying to get in contact
with you. Someone by the name of Shazad Ali,' Emily informed
him. 'Didn't like to pass on your mobile number without checking
with you first. He's on the club Board. He gave me his number
to pass on and said he would appreciate you ringing him urgently.
He also added at the end that he would appreciate it if you could
keep the matter confidential for the time being.'

From the way he raised his eyebrows in reaction, it was clear
to Emily it was not a call Frank had been expecting.

'What matter?' he questioned her.

'I'm not sure. I hoped you might know!' Again, she felt she had
acted wrongly. On reflection, it would have been a simple thing
for her to have checked with Shazad Ali whether the new Executive
Manager would know what 'matter' he was talking about.

'All sounds very mysterious, I'll say.' She was relieved to hear
him reply, with the hint of a colluding smile playing on his lips.

Not sure what else she could say, she passed him a note with
Shazad Ali's number on it.

'Thank you.'

As she was about to slip out of the room, she heard him call
out, 'Emily . . .'

'Yes, Mr Borrow?' she replied, in an unintended formal tone.

'Please, call me Frank. Do you mind if I ask you something?'

For a moment she stood there on tenterhooks, wondering what
on earth he was about to say.

67

'I don't want to put you on the spot, but would you happen to know how this Shazad Ali gets on with the Chair of the Board, Arnold Preston?'

From his hesitant manner, Emily could see he was uneasy putting such a question to her. The main problem though was, much as she would have liked to be able to pass on her opinion in a way that was helpful to him, she couldn't.

'I'm sorry Frank, I've no idea,' she answered completely honestly.

Of course he thought, suddenly taking stock, there was no reason why she should have even the faintest inkling. She had only started at the club on the day of his interview. What on earth was he doing putting her on the spot?

As Emily left, she could not deny feeling some quiet sense of satisfaction. It was nice that he had thought to ask her. She only wished in future he would ask her a question she knew something about!

9

Frank was heading towards Manchester without really knowing where he was going once he left the motorway. Despising the use of navigational aids, he belonged to the old-fashioned school of 'trial and error' in negotiating his route to any given destination.

From his brief preliminary phone conversation with Shazad Ali, apart from anything else Frank had got the picture of a technological whizz-kid who would have expected any self-respecting member of the human race to have the wits to find their way from a simple postcode using satnav or by whatever other means. On those grounds, Frank had felt a bit guilty asking for helpful nearby geographical landmarks to assist him in knowing when he was getting close to Shazad's place of business, enticingly called 'Shaz's Shangri-La'.

'Ask anyone in the area and they'll know where Shaz's Shangri-La is. You can't miss it if you follow signs towards Deansgate. Look out for Strangeways Prison on your immediate left. If you reach the cathedral you've gone too far. See you at 4.40, Frank. It's very good of you to agree to come out and see me at such short notice.'

Frank didn't need telling that, on his first day proper at work, he could have pleaded any number of pretexts to postpone this particular encounter. But although he couldn't quite put his finger on it, there must be benefit from picking up someone else's perceptions of where the club actually was and what might really be going on under the surface. Being on the Board, Shazad must be near to the heart of the operation.

The nagging doubt Frank had on each occasion he had heard Arnold Preston speak was that he wasn't getting anything like the full picture of what was happening. He feared more was being hidden than revealed. Of course, he couldn't have failed to pick up the disturbing tell-tale signs of a club under the cosh, with a poor league position behind them from the previous season, coupled with drastically declined ticket sales and the most recent disclosure that certain players were leaving the club for better prospects elsewhere.

While in normal circumstances Frank would have wasted no time in getting to grips with such problems, it seemed he had one arm tied behind his back at Oakhill United. As things stood, he had to work through, or at best round, the Manager and the Chair to try and make the kind of instant progress that seemed to be required at the club.

Hopefully, the meeting with Shazad Ali would be a useful exercise in enabling him to check out his hunches on someone else. However, on the question of the exact nature of 'the matter' Shazad was wishing to discuss with him so urgently, he had got no further on the phone in extracting any more detail. Frank would just have to be prepared to reserve judgement until they met face-to-face later in the day.

It always seemed the same when Ben came back from his father's. His self-esteem had taken another beating.

Not that, in her present frame of mind, Rosie felt altogether too much sympathy for her son. Contrary to the texts he had sent her saying he was staying overnight at his father's, her fraught memory from the night before had been of being forcibly awoken at some ungodly hour to the relentless sound of the hammering of fists on the front door.

Once she had collected her senses and worked out what was happening, she had switched the lights on and dashed down the two flights of stairs, putting her life at peril. Getting there quickly at least quelled the potential threat of irate comments from neighbours.

'Why didn't you use your blooming key to get in?' she had berated him. But he had had no proper answer, only muttering something about having 'lost' it. Because she could tell he was the worse for wear, it hadn't been worth challenging him further. Later, when she was turning out his pockets, she found the house key trapped in the lining.

All he seemed to want to do was go over why his father had decided to chuck him out of his house again. According to Ben, they had argued about a game of football they were watching on Sky. What had got to Ben was that, a year or so ago, his dad had seemed to respect his comments on a game. But Ben's take on things now was that, since he had been dropped from the academy, his dad openly scoffed at whatever he said.

Plausible as all this might have seemed, Rosie knew deep down that the relationship between them was so volatile that, if it hadn't been football, it could easily have been something else. But the net result was the same. Ben had been slung out on his ear. Rosie supposed the decision would have been endorsed by his dad's new woman as another example of firm, effective parenting.

Not surprising in the event that he'd left and got himself drunk. As usual, she was left picking up the pieces. Not that Ben showed any gratitude towards her for it. In his inebriated state, he even had the nerve to accuse her of being a bad mother. Where that came from, she could guess only too well! It just seemed these days she was becoming everyone's punchbag.

Then when Ben happens to let drop how much he's worried about whether he's going to be picked for more age-group trials taking place the following week at Oakhill United Academy, her brain feels like it is reeling. Not more crushing disappointment to put up with? She's not sure she can take it a second year running. While things were OK with Andy, the new guy seems clueless. She only wishes this new executive manager has more to do with the Academy. If he does, with his obviously greater all-round experience of the game, he will be bound to see how talented her son is . . .

'Found it all right then?'

'Yes the chimney is . . .' Frank didn't somehow manage to finish the sentence.

'Quite some phallic symbol, isn't it? Especially right in the middle of a male prison.'

The broad grin on the young man's face immediately suggested he wasn't one to pull punches.

'Well, how are you finding Oakhill United Football Club?' Shazad followed up, the grin subsiding slightly but by no means completely.

Frank supposed he could have come up with any number of bland responses, but there was a knowing expression on Shazad's face that told him it would be a waste of time to appear to dissemble.

'Let's call it a challenge.'

He could tell Shazad wasn't going to let him get away with that.

'But isn't that why you've been brought in? Look, let's face it; the place is in a mess. And it needs you to start kicking ass! That's my opinion, Mr Borrow, sir. Oh by the way I believe in getting down to brass tacks.'

'So where do I start then?' Frank found himself responding in playful but semi-provocative manner.

'Where would I start?' Shazad threw his head back in outright merriment. 'Do you really want to know? I'd start myself right at the top.'

'What, Simon Steele? That sounds a bit unfair.' Frank found himself unexpectedly on the defensive. 'I know he's young but he's not had much of a chance yet to prove himself . . .'

'Should never have been appointed in the first place! Whatever mistakes had been made in the past, the job was simply crying out for a man with experience. If I may be so bold as to say, like yourself.'

'Presumably though, you were on the appointment panel?'

'Was I hell? The Chair makes a point of keeping all that side to himself . . . and his hand-picked cronies! Anyway, I've only been on the Board six months. That's down to regulations saying there had to be a member of the business community on the Board.'

If Frank had been unsure whether Shazad was prepared to put his cards on the table, he needn't have worried. However closely Frank's views might match, there were obvious risks in allowing himself to sound too pally.

But Shazad was like a dog with a bone. 'No, I didn't mean Steele. I actually meant Preston needs to go. He's had a stranglehold on this club for far too long. Don't get me wrong, I like the man well enough and respect what he stands for. But he's not got the right approach towards the club at the present time, let alone for the future.'

My god, Shazad was getting down to brass tacks, all right! If he got any more direct, Frank would have no alternative but to head his car back down the motorway right away.

'So what was the specific matter you wished to raise?' He thought it best to try to return the conversation to practicalities. The young man looked back at him as if he was reacting obtusely or merely playing for time.

'Well, I suppose I'm raising it with you now, Mr Borrow. I don't think I can put it more bluntly, but in my view the club is ripe for a take-over and I intend to do everything I can to bring it about.'

'Why in particular do you feel it necessary to bring that to my attention?'

'Because you're the new man, aren't you?' the answer came back instantly. It was becoming quite amusing, particularly at his age, to hear himself described so often as 'the new man'.

'Yes, I suppose I am,' he duly acknowledged.

Shazad looked back at him with a serious air before continuing, 'You do know, if it had been left to Councillor Preston, the post you currently occupy would never have been agreed to in the first place?'

The directness of Shazad's gaze seemed to leave him with precious little room for manoeuvre.

'How do you know that?' Frank felt compelled to inquire.

'Well, because I put forward the motion myself that the club needed an executive manager with greater experience. I was flabbergasted that it got taken up. I think it must have been the first time in the history of Oakhill United that a vote was taken. Everything usually goes through on Arnold Preston's say-so as Chair of the Board.'

However intriguing all this sounded, Frank was beginning to feel very uncomfortable, and made as if to go. But Shazad was on too much of a roll.

'Let's face it, Arnold Preston is above all else a politician! He's got a vested interest in keeping the club an old-fashioned or so-called community club. The man even sees me as an outsider.'

'You as an outsider?' Frank offered back sympathetically.

'I don't mean in any obvious, racist way of course, more an outsider in terms of longstanding roots going back through centuries in the local area. Even so, I myself was born in Oakhill, as they say. Second generation. Actually, I've only been over to Pakistan once when I was six. Didn't like it. Took my GCSEs at a local comprehensive. Yes, my present business concern may be located in Manchester but I live in Oakhill. That's something Arnold Preston likes to ignore. The important thing is he's frightened stiff of anything that carries with it any sort of business tag.'

'Why is that?'

'Precisely because he fears a takeover. He knows I may not have enough clout myself. But a consortium is a different thing . . .'

A positive gleam came into Shazad's eye. 'That's another matter! You've seen the sheer number of wholesale outlets round here. Three or four of us combined could easily put up what's needed to take over financially. It's hardly Man United or Man City, is it? Even so, my view is there would be no stopping Oakhill United becoming a much bigger club if it had the right backing.'

'What would be your number one ambition for the club?' Frank found himself interested to ask.

'In the first instance, climbing out of League 2 by 2011.'

Inclined to show some residual loyalty to the present Chair of the Board, Frank felt bound to ask, 'Isn't that what Arnold Preston himself would want though?'

'Funny you ask, but I don't think so!'

'But why would any self-respecting chairman not want that?'

'I've heard Arnold Preston say many times that setting higher targets would only be storing up bigger problems for a later date.'

Suddenly Frank felt a strong sense of indignation. 'But that is ridiculous! As things stand, Oakhill United is ripe for the biggest fall that can happen to any club. Thrown out of the Football League altogether!'

'Now, you're talking, Mr Borrow! You see what I mean? Something has to be done.'

'From what I've seen, there has to be a radical turnover in the quality of players at the club.'

A philosophical look came over Shazad's face. 'Let's face it, Arnold Preston acts like it's a rest-home for long-serving players.'

Frank felt a natural instinct to say something to the effect that Shazad was being a bit harsh. But then, from his own admittedly slender evidence, it was a pretty accurate assessment.

'And another thing, while I'm on my soap box! If you take the Academy as a seed-bed for the club's future, I'd like to put to you a certain disturbing scenario. Now you may think I'm being biased here but it's this: Why don't young Asian lads ever manage to get into the club's Academy? Enough of them come for trial. Pitifully few ever get signed on! Yet football is very popular among the Asian population living in the area. You could do far worse, Mr Borrow, than to look at that aspect of what is happening at the club. On the face of it, 15-year-olds and 16-year-olds might not be high on the agenda but, believe me, they are the future of the club!'

Frank couldn't miss how passionate this young man was in his beliefs. But he also knew that he couldn't allow himself to be unduly swayed. He needed time to go away and assimilate what he was hearing.

At the end of their meeting, Frank felt he owed it to Shazad to be as honest as possible. 'I will take serious account of what you've said. You will though need to give me time to see what I make of things. But of one thing you can be sure, I will not be afraid to speak up candidly when the time comes.'

'That sounds most reasonable, if you don't mind my saying so.' As Frank got up to go, Shazad said, almost by way of apology, 'By the way, I hope you don't mind meeting me in my humble office. I trust I haven't lost face by not taking you out to some posh, swanky hotel in central Manchester. But from my own point of view, I'd rather show you where I work so that you can see me for myself and where I'm coming from: blood, sweat and tears!'

'Not at all,' said Frank, having noticed ironically that Shazad's office space was by the front entrance and in full view of everyone who might visit Shaz's Shangri-La.

As Frank drove back onto the main road, his final thoughts were that he couldn't really disagree with anything he had heard. Yet the most challenging aspect was how to tackle what needed doing. Whatever he said about needing a bit of time, it didn't really look like he was going to have that luxury!

10

Frank had been hoping fairly soon he and Simon would be able to have a meeting together with the club captain, John Appleton. But when John had called in on him of his own accord on the second day back, Frank recognised it would have appeared uncivil to turn him away.

Proud to announce to Frank that the start of this new season marked his seventh at Oakhill United, John went on to say confidingly, 'There are a lot of us here who form the backbone of the present team, who were signed on at the same time by Matt Hewson. We've kind of grown together . . .'

As John was talking, Frank was reminded of the fact that the only team photo hanging up in the changing rooms was one from 2006–7 with Hewson sitting on the front row. Yes, it hadn't escaped Frank's attention that many of the players in that photo were still at the club. On the face of it, there was nothing wrong with that. Lots of clubs did well from building teams round a well-established group of players. However, the only trouble in Oakhill United's case was that the club had not been doing too well at all in recent times with the type of players John was referring to.

With a slightly preaching edge to his voice, John continued: 'This club has always done more than just treat us as ordinary footballers. It's been a club that has nurtured our professional development. We're very grateful for that.'

John paused as if giving a chance for this fulsome testimony to sink in. For his part, though, Frank couldn't quite grasp the significance of the point being made. Perhaps there wasn't one. Except he could sense that some kind of marking of his card was going on. It was of course what you might expect when you were new to a club. It wasn't just his visit to Manchester to see Shazad Ali that fell into this category.

As John shaped to go on, Frank hoped things would become more transparent.

'That's something the Chair of the Board has always been enthusiastic to foster too. It's about players feeling valued which probably explains why so many of the core players are happy here and never look to move to any other club.'

Picking up the message loud and clear, it was impossible for Frank to miss the utter complacency oozing out of every pore! I'll bet everyone's happy here, he thought, they've never had any real demands placed on them. Very much feeling like saying something to that effect, Frank bit his lip and just smiled back, as though grateful for having these pearls of wisdom bestowed upon him by the club captain.

He had ended up by thanking John for his time and assuring him that Simon and he would be very keen to meet with him for a further talk on where the club was heading this season.

As things stood, based on John's present interpretation, it would probably be heading out of existence. The final, unflattering thought in Frank's mind was to wonder which other club on earth would dream of taking on any of the players who made up the so-called 'backbone' of Oakhill United?

Frank had let it be known that he intended to spend his first week at Oakhill observing. It seemed vital to audit the present state of affairs at the club. Simon had responded to the approach with a neutral look on his face, probably a bit relieved in one sense that the other man wasn't diving in to take over from the outset. But Frank appreciated Simon would realise he wouldn't just be making assessments about players, but also on the other man's own ability as a manager.

He appreciated the players were bound to have a reaction too. Usually, on past occasions of doing something similar at a new club, he'd found it went one of two ways. At the better-run clubs he could think back to, players took it as natural and were hell-bent from the start to show themselves at their very best in terms of work rate and general performance. At other types of clubs he'd gone to, a definite sense of unease, perhaps with a fear factor, had marked the players' response.

Here at Oakhill it had already become clear that the reaction was more disturbing than anything he had encountered before. The players here weren't just concerned about being put under a spotlight, they actively resented it!

Although of course they didn't really have much option, Frank could see they were sceptical about being put under any kind of scrutiny. This was conspicuously the case with the type of players who John Appleton had called the core or backbone of the team. Defying Frank's disbelief, it seemed they expected him blindly to sympathise and get behind them from the word go, completely forgoing any more critical element to his own role. Of course, all of this was bound to focus Frank's mind back on what Simon had been doing, or not doing, to establish a necessary agenda for improvement. For however much he was prepared to continue making allowance for the fact it was his first year in management, it was already beginning to hit Frank between the eyes that there was no way he himself could fudge issues at Oakhill United.

The inevitable consequence was that he recognised he would fairly soon need to take positive action in seeking to take Simon along with him. If he had been on his own, it would of course have been more simple. Adding to Frank's burdens was the distinct ongoing impression that Simon remained intent on blocking him as much as he possibly could. Bending over backwards to be fair, Frank couldn't fault Simon's sense of commitment, for example through unfailingly being first on and last off club premises each and every day of the week. As Frank could readily recall from his own first job, if you lacked the experience, you were doubly determined to make up for it in terms of putting in the hours.

For one reason or another, Frank could appreciate no real obvious need had yet arisen for him to spell out his own take on things to Simon. However, everything under the surface seemed to be pushing him in that inevitable direction. Knowing how prickly Simon had proved to this point, Frank hoped any ensuing conversation would end up more as a meeting of minds than a direct confrontation . . .

'Hi, I'm Matt. I'm in charge of our academy. Pleased to meet you!'

'Likewise,' Frank assured him as he rose from his desk to shake the young man's hand.

'Sorry I haven't managed to introduce myself before but I was on my annual leave when you were appointed,' Matt explained engagingly. 'Look, boss, you'll be up to your neck first week, I bet, but if there's any chance of catching a few minutes with you sometime to talk about how you see the future of the academy, I'd really appreciate it.'

Frank caught a slight worried look on Matt's face when he referred to 'the future' of the academy. The least he felt he could do in return was to say something to instil a sense of confidence.

'I want you to know I fully believe the future of any club first and foremost depends on the quality of the young players coming through at academy level.'

Whether he fully believed this or not, it was amazing what power a few well-chosen words could have. Matt's face broke out instantly into a beaming smile. 'You mean you're not thinking of axing the academy straight away then?'

'Exactly as I said. But like any other part of the club, we'll have to see what can be done to improve things wherever possible.'

'Yes, my attitude precisely.' Then, presumably aimed at

impressing 'the new man'. 'We run a busy programme all year round. In fact, trials for new young players are taking place this coming week.'

A nerve-end twitched somewhere in Frank's head, as something Shazad Ali had said echoed uncomfortably in his mind. 'Just as a matter of interest, are there any Asians putting themselves forward?'

'I've got the list here. Let me see, it's the 15-year-old age group. Of course we already have a lot of players on our books. But it's always good to do a fresh trawl at the start of the year. Here, have a look yourself. I'm sorry it looks a bit rough. Call it a working document!'

Frank studied the sheet which comprised a list of names with ticks and crosses against them. About thirty names in all with about half of them ticked. His eye scanned the list. One Bashir, two Khans and a Mahmood – one tick, three crosses.

'How do you decide which lads to bring along?'

'Obviously, I take into account school reports. We also like though to know what kind of support there is at home. That can be a very important factor at this young age.'

Following through to the end of the alphabetical list, Frank had his attention caught by the sight of one name towards the end, Ben Skipton. The name showed a cross against it.

'If lads get rejected, is it possible for them to be reconsidered at a later time?'

Matt looked back, puzzled, not sure what the other man was driving at. No doubt he was wondering what he had let himself in for with this unexpected grilling over detail.

'Look, if you're interested, boss, why not come along to the trials and take a look for yourself? You'd be more than welcome. It'd give the lads an extra buzz.'

'Have the invitations to the trials gone out yet?'

'No, as I said, these are just my first workings-out. They'll not be going out till tomorrow.'

What felt like an inspirational idea burst into Frank's mind.

'In the best interests of looking an inclusive club, why don't we invite them all? What's the harm in that?'

'No harm at all, boss. Whatever you say . . .'

Although it was Friday evening and the end of a hard first week at the club, there was still more than enough preying on Frank's mind. He supposed he could take some comfort from the fact he'd now completed his preliminary observation schedule. The only trouble was that with a rapidly extending list of priorities to tackle, it was becoming almost impossible for him to know where to begin.

He had hoped to check out his perceptions at the end of the week with Simon. But, try as he might, it had not proved possible. Perhaps it was his own fault for not formally arranging a time to do so. Mistakenly, as it turned out, he had somehow thought Simon might be interested to hear what he had made of the week. Or at least be prepared to shift things around in his diary that Friday afternoon. But not a bit of it! On the other hand, Frank appreciated just how vulnerable Simon might still be feeling on his own account. Avoidance at all costs could yet have remained the safer-sounding option to him.

Thinking of positive ways of moving forward for the benefit of the club's prospects for the new season, the main thing Frank had wanted to run by Simon, before the end of the week, was the possibility of attracting players to the club to fill the obvious holes left by the departures of Brown, Marrison and Pierce. These three players, two midfielders and one striker, had provided Oakhill with virtually the whole of its attacking fire-power. Without them, it was obvious to any practised eye, the team totally lacked players with the ability to create or score goals. In other words, Oakhill United was a dead duck! Simon Steele could talk in prospect about one or two home-grown young lads who might be given the chance to step in, but Frank suspected he himself knew they were nowhere near ready to fill the other men's boots. Simon had discouragingly added that he felt his own hands were tied in the matter. This was because he believed he would necessarily have to wait until the next board meeting in a fortnight's time to ask permission to sign on any new players.

Frank had to take action! The alternatives were all unthinkable. Within ten minutes of arriving home, he was on the phone to Tony Bennison and Paul Carpenter, two players from his last club. Aware they would both be unhappy that new players had been signed on in their positions, Frank knew they would be open to temptation. Both good players, they were bound to be considerable assets to Oakhill United. In the event, it hadn't called for silky persuasive skills to entice them over the following Monday to discuss signing-on terms. Come hell or high water, he felt he had to take action to rescue Oakhill United Football Club from the abyss. Anything else seemed like a bonus.

Emily had received the following text from Martin:

> *You'd have loved the exhibition. It epitomised the bleakness of the northern landscape and can't help but bring the viewer into closer touch with his or her innermost soul.*

Emily had felt guilty turning down Martin's kind invitation to tea, followed by a viewing of an exhibition of watercolour paintings commissioned for the museum where he worked as curator. Pleased as she was to hear him sounding in raptures, nothing in his text had caused her to regret her decision to stay at home.

If it had been on a Saturday rather than a Friday evening, she might have felt more in the mood. But working full-time at Oakhill seemed to be taking its toll. All she usually felt like doing was slumping down on the settee, indulging in a glass of wine or two and watching something undemanding on TV. Friday night was positively the last time she wished to have her 'innermost soul' probed. She would have come away feeling positively suicidal.

Besides she'd have had to mingle with people and engage in all that kind of footling small talk which she associated with dreadful cocktail parties. If she was being honest, even though she hadn't said this to Martin when making her excuses, she much preferred the idea of going along with him to an occasion like a play or an opera. In those settings, she knew in advance she could relax in her seat, cocooned in a dark auditorium, and just watch as the story unfolded.

Although she appreciated it was selfishness on her part, for which she roundly recriminated herself, she much preferred going somewhere with Martin when he himself had to be quiet, rather than having chance to prattle on about his hobby-horses in the art world.

In actual fact, contrary to her normal mode of wallowing in self-indulgence on a Friday night, she had brought home with her something from work which she was very interested in. Frank Borrow had given her the job of typing up the copious notes he had compiled from his week-long observation exercise. From some of the vibes she'd picked up during the week, she anticipated it might make for quite lively reading. Sad, she knew, to admit this! Snatching a quick Caesar salad and uncorking a bottle of her favourite Prosecco, she'd even sneaked a look at it then, catching the immediate sense that it didn't pull any punches. She wondered how well it was going to be received by the players, who he assessed were only doing about half the amount of training and gym work needed to be properly fit. The legibility of Frank's handwriting had given her a slight sense of panic. Presumably professors, like doctors, were so immersed in what they were doing that they didn't bother about less important matters like the neatness of their writing. Having said that, Emily was quite looking forward to spending time that evening getting on with it.

Proof-reading her work later on, she sniggered at the thought that Simon Steele would probably have a heart attack. Particularly when he read one or two of the more ground-breaking recommendations which came at the end. That is, assuming that Frank was able to break into his office to gain an audience. Pouring herself another glass of Prosecco as a reward for her efforts, she knew she didn't know much about football, but she reckoned she could always tell when a bust-up was round the corner.

11

In case he might oversleep, Frank had set his alarm clock to go off at 5 o'clock that Monday morning. But in the event he needn't have worried. His mind had been racing so much with thoughts of the coming week that he knew he wouldn't have to depend on it. Sleep had been a non-starter. Sitting bolt upright in his bed, he watched the luminous numbers on the clock laboriously wind forward, like waiting for the whistle to go at the end of a dull game.

Instantly switching off the buzzer, but feeling philosophical about putting the sleepless night behind him, he had arisen sharply to prepare himself his customary muesli breakfast topped with fruit, nuts and yoghurt. He realised it had been asking a lot of Emily to spend extra hours over the weekend knocking his scruffy notes into shape. But there hadn't been any real alternative if he was going to be ready, as planned, to hit the ground running at the start of the second week. Not that he had exactly demanded the task be carried out. Having said that, he had been mightily relieved when she appeared to accede to his request so willingly. At the same time he had made a mental note not to assume too readily again in the future that everybody must be like himself, with nothing else to do at the weekend.

He'd asked Emily if she could make it into the office as early as possible, and she had again duly obliged. To her credit, she had suggested emailing it but he was still too unconfident about the set-up in his house to take up the offer. Besides, she would find out fairly soon, he was a technological dunce.

Apart from anything else which prompted Frank to get to work early, he had an impulse to break his duck by arriving before Simon Steele. Not that this was simply one-upmanship. It was just that it had begun to irritate Frank that, however early he had arrived in the previous week, Simon always seemed to be there first, smugly stationed at his desk. Worse than that, it was obvious he been there some time already. It was as if Frank was late in! Of course, it was a commendable trait in the young man to want to be getting down to things early. Although he could never be sure what Simon was doing, it seemed he was always busy picking up and dispatching email messages to all and sundry.

Frank had an impulse to buck the trend this morning. Call it mind games or whatever, he felt a vital need to make his mark by being in pole position at the start of the week.

So far, so good then! By the time he had scooped the empty muesli bowl into the dishwasher, shaved and got dressed, he was still on target, even making allowances for the heavy morning traffic. His objective was to arrive at work no later than 7 o'clock.

No sooner had he locked the front door behind him and turned to climb into his car than, out of the corner of his eye, he snatched an unexpected glimpse of a red sports car coasting along Queen Anne's Way and about to pass his house. Rosie Skipton's car.

Bearing in mind his existing state of resolve, it would surely have sufficed for him to acknowledge his street-neighbour with a mere wave of the hand. But, for whatever reason, he had flagged her down as if she was caught in a speed trap.

She had brought the car to a halt within inches of where he was standing. Winding down the window, the expression on her face was one of surprise with also a look of expectation that he might have something fairly pressing to say. But unable to grasp what he had just done, he stared at her numbly. The best he could lamely come up with, to hide his embarrassment, was, 'Oh, I see your car is back on the road then?'

'Yes, it is,' she replied matter-of-factly and then smiled as if touched by his concern on her behalf. 'This week looks more promising all round!'

'Oh?' he said, unable to think what she might be referring to.

'Ben has been invited for trial again at Oakhill! It's fantastic news! You ought to see the difference it's made to him in his outlook?' Her face positively beamed up at him.

As she continued to explain how much Ben was looking forward to doing his best on the Wednesday, Frank didn't feel the need to reply but just went on bathing in the warmth of her smile.

It was 7.17 when he finally managed to reach the Oakhill United Football Club car park. Like Captain Scott seeing the Norwegian flag hoisted up at the South Pole, his heart sank to see Simon Steele's car there ahead of him.

Oh well, there was always tomorrow to try again in that direction . . . but one way or another, he was definitely intent on making his mark today.

When Emily arrived in the office, it had surprised her to hear what sounded like a very heated conversation going on in Simon's office. At first she couldn't tell who might be in there with him. Whoever it was, it wasn't just Simon's voice that was audible. Then, in the next instant, the penny dropped. She hadn't anticipated things getting combustible that quickly.

No, the way she had visualised it was that Frank would decide to keep his powder dry at least until fully armed with his report and recommendations in their final form. Besides, wasn't that why he had asked her in earlier, so that he could check it all through? Discomfortingly, she could hear everything as if inside the room herself. She supposed it was only to be expected that Simon would adopt his familiar stance.

'Look, you know damned well how I feel! I've had nowhere near enough time yet to get to grips with all the problems there are at this club. If I'd known when I'd joined, I'd seriously have thought twice about taking the job. But I do know exactly what

those problems are and, believe me, I intend making the necessary changes to deal with them!'

After a short pause, she heard Frank's voice in a heavy, measured and deliberate tone responding.

'Do you mind me asking, Simon? Do you envisage making
those changes before or after the club is presented with its winding-
up order?'

The logic behind the question seemed unanswerable. She imagined Simon was bound to be squirming under the pressure of it.
She knew she would have been. But his reply appeared to suggest
he had either missed the point or else he was determined to go
on holding onto the ropes and riding the blows: 'Look, this is my
first job. I know I haven't got your experience. I'm feeling my
way. First, I have to win the players' respect. I'm biding my time.
Then I'll make the tough decisions that need making . . .'

And then as if something had given him a nudging reminder
of the question that had been put to him, she heard Simon say
in a more thoughtful way, 'I realise you have the experience and
you must know more about these things, Frank. But I can't possibly
think matters are that serious.'

Another pause. Then in an even more deliberate tone, the
answer came: 'Yes they fucking well are!'

There was a silence as if the air had been cut with a knife.
Although it wasn't for her to say, she was shocked. It somehow
jolted her to think that Frank would speak in such terms. Clearly,
though, there must be a side to him she hadn't quite taken account
of.

'The way things are going, how soon do you think?' she heard
Simon's voice suddenly sounding almost subdued.

'Much sooner than later! Any time in the next month or so,
if we don't act instantly to put things right.'

'Well, what do you suggest then?'

'I suggest you and I spend an hour going through what I came
up with in the way of findings from last week. Then we agree
on putting together an agenda. However, we can't afford to waste

any more time. We need to talk to the players and I think we should call a meeting with them this morning. At that meeting, we break the news to them that the way things get done around here is going to have to get a lot sharper.'

'OK, I'm with that,' she was stunned to hear Simon say in agreement. 'First, though do you mind if I tell the PA to get us some coffee or maybe something stronger? I'll tell her to call the players together at 10.'

As the door opened, she heard Simon call back in a tone that sounded collaborative, almost matey, 'It's all right for you, Frank, at your age. You can afford to walk away from all this. I've still got twenty-six years to pay on my fucking mortgage!'

Although it had been said in her direct hearing, she found herself smiling. At least the two of them were now speaking the same language.

'May I start by sharing with you some of the strengths I saw last week?'

As he'd hoped, this method of opening his analysis seemed to succeed in striking a positive chord with the players. At least they were hearing him speak this time, unlike the previous occasion when the Chair of the Board had hogged proceedings throughout. The playing staff of Oakhill FC seemed visibly to relax. By god though, he realised only too well this section of so-called 'strengths' wasn't set to last too long!

'First of all, in defence we have a solid base to build on. We have a truly excellent keeper and two dependable centre-backs.' How to win friends and influence people! The three players in question picked up on the vibes, clearly intent on dining out on such praise.

'Moving on to midfield then . . .' Frank paused, if only as a means of enabling the more discerning to register he had failed to make any reference to either of the highly dubious full-backs. Such subtlety wasn't lost for one moment on the two players in question, who could be seen exchanging meaningful glances.

'As I said, moving on to midfield . . .' Again he paused, but this time it was because he found it impossible to identify any inherent strengths whatsoever. Without the two midfield players who had gone, Brown and Marrison, it was patently clear the engine of the team had been ripped out. But he had to say something, even just for appearances' sake. Didn't he? Only the best he had been able to muster was: 'We are at our best in midfield when we pass the ball accurately and seek to close down the opposition when they're in possession.'

Hardly a priceless accolade was it? Although he didn't care much to enlarge, the truth was that the midfield players remaining at the club were very rarely capable of demonstrating either the skills or even the basic determination to carry out these minimal requirements.

'As for our strike force . . .' Again, the words seemed to fail him. Another significant pause in which to try and conjure up something positive to say. 'We don't lack effort chasing after the ball. The only problem is . . .'

Oh no! Hadn't he said he was concentrating on the actual strengths? Yet here he was, barely sixty seconds later, directly homing in on the whole rag-bag of wretched weaknesses. There seemed no alternative but to put it baldly: 'In all the practices I attended throughout last week, at no time did we look capable of scoring a single goal.'

There, he had gone and said it! Perhaps it was stretching it to go on and say, 'The truth is that, without Pierce, the front line is as toothless as a shareholder in Steradent.'

There you have it, he felt like saying, only the aggrieved look on every face in the audience suggested he would be well advised to move on quickly.

'So where do we go from here?' he posed the question, supremely confident he had the appropriate answers up his sleeve.

During the half-hour that followed, he made no bones about telling them where they were going from here. He knew in advance they wouldn't like the medicine. Not at first anyway. But there was nothing at all in his view to be gained by attempting to sugar the pill.

Two things he went on to say probably helped avoid an instant riot or walk-out. One was that he was only giving them his honest assessment. The second was that he didn't want Oakhill to go out of the Football League and into extinction.

'Is there anyone here who wants to see the club kicked out of the league?' There was clearly a rhetorical, provocative edge to the question, he knew, but Frank's approach was to let anyone come out of the woodwork who was intent on blocking him.

None of the players moved a muscle. But he had only just started the brow-beating.

'Because if there is anyone here who does, I may as well bugger off back to where I came from.'

Now he was talking the language. Even the senior players started sitting up in their seats. They'd heard the vernacular before of course. It was stock in trade. That was why he saved his use of more bruising language for the moment of greatest impact. It lost its effect if used every third word. But he sensed he had them going.

'Simon Steele may as well bugger off. The lot of us may as well just pack our bags now.'

It wasn't so much a matter of whether he was going to touch a few raw nerves, but when. He could tell the moment was upon him, the make-or-break defining moment to get his point across in a way that took on the troops but didn't brook dissent. No quarter asked, none given, the type of approach he would in time demand from them on the field of play.

'What is it we need to do then?' By this point Frank knew he had a fair measure of control over his audience. Nodding in the other man's direction for support, he went on: 'Simon and I had a long talk this morning and we agreed we need to do the following.'

He didn't want to labour the point to the players that he and Simon had talked things over already, but it was important they heard that the two of them were working together and agreed on a new regime.

'Two main changes to begin with. First of all, we're holding a team talk everyday to make sure everyone knows what we're setting out to achieve on a day-to-day basis.

'Secondly, training will take place now morning and afternoon, not just mornings, as at the moment. Is everyone clear?'

The second element, as Frank had expected, caused a considerable stir. It was club captain John Appleton who took it upon himself to give a first take: 'But many of us do valuable work in the area in the afternoons like visiting schools. Does that mean we have to give up on all that side?'

Frank took stock for a second. It wasn't the time to be giving any leeway. Not one inch.

'What are we? A football club or a community self-help scheme?'

Detecting quite a lot of reaction to this latest shot across the bows, he heard John Appleton fire a torpedo back. 'That work in the afternoon does a lot to get the area of Oakhill behind the team, Mr Borrow.'

He was going to have to take this on, wasn't he?

'Do you think that reflects in numbers of advance season tickets sold, John?'

The club captain hesitated.

'Do you know how many have been sold this year?' Frank unashamedly paused for effect. 'Seven hundred! Do you know how many had been sold last year at the same stage?' Again the pause . . . 'Three thousand five hundred.'

Appleton's torpedo was blown out of the water!

'That's it then gentlemen. The new programme starts tomorrow.'

As the players trooped out, it suddenly occurred to Frank that he hadn't yet mentioned to Simon that Tony Bennison and Paul Carpenter were due to appear at midday. It would be interesting to see the effect this had on the players. If any of them thought it was going to be the same as last season they had another think coming.

12

'Did anyone stand out for you in particular, boss?' Matt Johnson gently inquired after the pair of them had finished watching two hours of academy trials on the Wednesday afternoon.

Despite the eagerness of the prompt, Frank thought it best not to jump in. 'One or two . . . what did you think?' he replied, preferring to reserve his own judgement until he had heard what Matt had to say.

'I always ask myself the same question. Did I see anyone who's better than those we already have in our squad?'

Frank sensed he could predict what the answer was going to be. 'And . . .?'

'To be honest, I don't think I did.'

If that was the criterion, Frank was bound to be at a disadvantage since he hadn't yet seen any of the current squad. He thought the timing right to assert his own thoughts.

'What about Skipton? He looked to have everything a left-sided midfielder needs, very tricky going forward, a good eye for an opening, tracked back well and above all else, a great ability to read the game.'

'That's some recommendation if you don't mind me saying. I can see all that, but . . .'

'But?'

'I can't argue that you saw Skipton at his best on this occasion, but . . .' This time, Frank kept silent, waiting for Matt to commit himself to stating the reservation he so obviously harboured.

'It has to be said he's been in our academy squad before and . . . how can I put it? He never seemed to fit in. Besides, there are one or two other factors pretty well known around the place.'

It strongly appeared to Frank that the other man wasn't just referring to things that took place on the football field.

'You're making it sound like he has a drug problem or something?'

'No, not that I know of.'

'Well, what then?'

'If you really want to know.' Matt clearly appeared awkward about proceeding but felt obliged now to explain. 'It never made things any easier that his mother seemed, it was widely believed, to have my predecessor Andy . . . how can I put this delicately? . . . dangling on the end of a string!'

This 'Andy' of course, it suddenly connected up in Frank's mind, was the one who had previously occupied his own house on Queen Anne's Way.

'None of it particularly went down well with the parents of other players in the squad. Rightly or wrongly, they thought Ben got preferential treatment on the back of the "relationship", shall we call it? Ultimately Andy left under something of a cloud but it didn't stop the tongues wagging. In fact, I particularly remember the way one mother made a special point of warning me about Ben's mother, telling me she was "all fur coat and no knickers"!'

It was as if Matt had expected Frank to be amused by his anecdote. But Frank's stony indifference to what he was being told did nothing to encourage him. The quiet chuckle that had been playing around Matt's lips froze immediately.

'That's very interesting indeed, I'm sure!' was how Frank had responded dismissively. He wasn't going to risk his own dignity by saying he had already met Ben's mother but had gained an altogether different impression. Instead he decided it was fair time to demonstrate to Matt the importance of keeping their minds firmly on the actual question of footballing ability rather than allowing empty rumour to enter into the equation. On that basis, feeling even more strongly a need to express his opinion, Frank asserted: 'In my view, Ben Skipton was head and shoulders above anyone else in that trial. In fact, for a 15-year-old, I'd go so far as to say he's a phenomenal prospect. Probably better than anyone else I've seen playing in the first team in that position.'

Matt looked discomfited as though he still needed to justify himself for what he had let slip. 'I agree, but I hope you can see where I was coming from. I just thought I'd better tell you the other stuff going on in people's minds around here.'

'But this Andy has gone now. So that's surely all over and done with.'

'Yes, boss,' the other man humbly conceded.

'My own view is that we have at all costs to base our judgements on the ability of players. Pure and simple.'

'OK. So we take young Skipton back into the academy then?'

'Most certainly!'

Regardless of anything else, Frank was determined that, from the start of this second week onwards, he should go on handling all matters arising at the club as firmly and singlemindedly as possible.

Emily ought to have learnt by now that, when she was trying to impress her nephew Tom with what was going on at Oakhill United, she always seemed to get slightly more than she bargained for.

'It hardly sounds in the same league as Real Madrid signing on Ronaldo and Kaka!' This had been Tom's superior response to her crowing that Oakhill had signed two good players, Bennison and Carpenter. Not that she'd even heard of Kaka. She could place Ronaldo because, when he'd been playing for Manchester United, he'd always seemed to be on the front page crashing cars and chasing women.

'How many millions did the two at Oakhill cost?' Tom had followed up whimsically. She refused to let him wring it out of her. It would only have humiliated her to have to accept they'd been brought in on free transfers. Twigging far too late, she realised she should have waited until Tom's dad was around. With his seemingly encyclopaedic footballing knowledge, he would no doubt have known something about their past heroic deeds.

Leaving all this aside, Emily had noticed the two signings had put a fresh spring in Frank's step. It was obviously a big boost to him being reunited with two players he was familiar with and rated highly. Even so, she suspected there might have been some friction with Simon over the signings. Although Frank had made sure he introduced the players to him straight after their arrival on the Monday, she could tell from the look of astonishment on Simon's face that the matter came as a bit of a revelation. What did it say that Frank was acting so quickly and decisively to add new players to the squad?

However uncertain Simon might still have felt, Emily had picked up a more immediate reaction from Jack Hubbard. When Frank had called in the press to do a piece and a photo-shoot of the two players, resplendent in full Oakhill United regalia, she had overheard Jack mutter, 'I don't know where the new man thinks the brass is coming from to pay their wages!'

With her business hat on, she could understand where Jack was coming from. For he was the one in the daily firing-line of the auditors and reeling under the pressure. At least he had swallowed his pride and accepted her offer of assistance this time around. However, the more she came to learn about the state of the club's finances, the more dire was the overall picture emerging.

A major problem the auditors had already identified was that in no proper sense did the club have a business plan to work on. Jack formulated financial spending plans at the start of the season and drew up end-of-season balance sheets. Presumably the Board monitored affairs on an ongoing basis in mid-season meetings. But, apart from airy resolves in the so-called 'Statement of Intent', the club had no realistic costed plans or defined objectives. This matter was going to need addressing urgently if the club wasn't to descend into an even worse predicament.

Only today, she had sat through a very uncomfortable meeting with the auditors. At one point Jack had seemed as if he were about to make some sharp comment in Frank's direction but had chosen to bite his lip instead. Then, after the meeting when the auditors had gone, Jack had rounded on Frank. 'How do you think we're going to pay the wages of these new players?'

'I assumed we'd be able to afford them out of the savings made from Brown, Marrison and Pierce going,' Frank had responded.

'Those "savings" are needed to reduce existing debts!' Jack had rapped back at him.

'Have you not heard the phrase strike while the iron is hot?'

'All I can say,' Jack had fired back, 'is that you'd better save up your ammunition for the Board meeting in two weeks' time!'

When Arnold Preston picked up his evening copy of *The Oakhill Times*, his eyes skimmed over the front-page headline: *NO TO NEW SUPERMARKET*!

However much the local paper liked to make its daily lead sound like a scoop to its readers, it was very rare indeed over the years for them to come up with anything that he himself did not know about already. True to form, the story tonight about an application for a new supermarket being turned down was an issue he had been closely involved with over a period of months in his councillor capacity. He wouldn't have said the plan had foundered completely on the back of his own personal efforts but, bearing in mind he had orchestrated opposition behind the scenes, he could take a lot of quiet satisfaction from seeing the final outcome laid bare on the front page.

As he flicked desultorily through the rest of the paper, he had seen nothing much else to capture his attention until coming across the headline on the very back page in the sports section: *YES TO NEW PLAYERS!*

Underneath the headline there was a picture showing two players. Although the Oakhill kit they were wearing was instantly recognisable, the so-called newcomers themselves, by the names of Tony Bennison and Paul Carpenter, meant absolutely nothing to him. Staring aghast, he was confounded by the thought that two players should have been signed without him knowing, let alone a deal being struck that hadn't met with his approval or that of the Board. His initial thought was almost one of relief that the press hadn't been on to him, as they so often were on footballing as well as political issues, because it would have been cringingly embarrassing to have to confess he knew nothing about it.

Within a matter of seconds he was hot on the phone and tearing into Simon Steele: 'What the hell is this piece on the back page about two new players?'

All he could hear back was a muffled, awkward silence.

'Hello?' Arnold pressed.

'Hello. Yes . . . er, two new players have been signed.'

'I can see that for myself! May I remind you of club protocols? The manager is entitled to make recommendations about new players. It is then totally the prerogative of the Board to approve any recommendations or not. I thought you knew that Simon?'

'Frank Borrow signed them up.'

'Oh, did he now?'

'I kind of assumed he must have run it by you, Chairman.' And then almost as an afterthought, 'I didn't get to know myself until Frank brought them round to the club on Monday. By the way, they're from the last club he was at.'

'I'm not sure I'm getting an altogether clear picture in my head about this, Simon. Are you telling me Frank did this completely independently?'

'Well, yes, I suppose I am.'

'All I can say is I'm going to have to think about this very seriously. For the time being at least, it may be best if you didn't share it with Frank Borrow that we've had this conversation. But I have to say I find it deeply insulting, as Chairman of the Board, that I've not only not been consulted but have then been put through the indignity of finding out about it through the local rag! It appears from what you say that Frank Borrow is wholly responsible but let me tell you, Simon, I expect you to keep me fully informed of what is going on in future.'

'Yes indeed, Councillor Preston.'

After the conversation had finished, however hard he felt he had been put through his paces, Simon was glad he had had a chance to clarify his own stance on the matter. If anything, he felt it had reinforced his position with the Chair. Of course, unless things should dramatically change for whatever reason, he knew his core loyalty had to lie with the man who had appointed him. After all, as he always had to remind himself at such critical moments, he still had a heck of a huge amount to pay back on his mortgage.

Given the mood Jack had been in after the meeting with the auditors, Frank hadn't cared, let alone dared, to tell him more about the transactions he had carried out involving Tony Bennison and Paul Carpenter. It boiled down to the fact that the only way he had been able to entice the two players from his former club across to Oakhill was by offering them terms and conditions of employment way over and above the ones they were on presently. With Carpenter, a happy-go-lucky but very useful striker in his late 20s, it had been straightforward enough to lure him with an offer of considerably more per week than his present wage.

But in the other player's case the matter had been a good deal more complex. Bennison had been an outstanding midfielder in his prime, playing for most of his career at Premier League level until only four years ago. Like a lot of players having an eye for the future, he had collected all his FA coaching badges and taken every opportunity to gain experience in management. Now he was seeking to reap the dividends.

With Frank's backing, Tony had spent time the previous summer in South Africa, one of Frank's own stamping grounds. Particularly with the whole country buzzing at the prospect of shortly staging the World Cup finals, it had provided a fantastic stage for Tony to learn the ropes of management. At the time, it had made Frank feel enormously nostalgic. Of course, his own time out there had been at a far less propitious period prior to the watershed of 1992 when the Fifa Congress had re-admitted South Africa into the international fold following the release of Mandela and the end of apartheid. Most of the black clubs that Frank had been used to working with in those former times hadn't even had their own grounds to play on. The dictat of the previous regime had been to restrict black ownership of anything whatsoever. Not to digress, but he couldn't help feeling an even stronger affinity to Tony for the mere fact that he seemed somehow to be keen to be following in his footsteps . . .

Definitely though, Tony still had at least two years to offer as a player. At a League 2 club like Oakhill United, probably more. But Frank had never sought to persuade players just to go on for the sake of longevity. At the very outside, he anticipated Tony striving to make the transition to becoming a player-manager in a year's time. Although Frank had tried to spell out to Tony all the inherent difficulties in attempting to combine such a difficult dual role, he knew it was still in the young man's mindset to go for such a job, probably at a top non-league club in this country or even perhaps abroad.

At some point very soon though, Frank was going to have to take it upon himself to square all this with Simon: that one of the terms he had worked out with Tony was that he should be able to take on a significant coaching position as well as a central midfield role as a player. It had even dawned on Frank that if Simon Steele hadn't been already in situ, it would have proved a far more agreeable 'double act' if he had gone to Oakhill United with Tony Bennison in the first place. As it was, though, Frank now not only had to deal with all the difficulties from Simon feeling threatened, but he also had somehow to establish Tony in a coaching role without rocking the boat.

Meanwhile, Frank could console himself that Tony was bound

to prove immensely valuable as a player, both in his own right and also as a role model for others around him in the team. His spirit of total dedication had already proved tremendously useful to Frank after the decision taken earlier in the week to double the amount of training time. While the club captain, John Appleton, always appeared to be pacing himself, Tony Bennison conspicuously threw himself in at the deep end and never-endingly encouraged others to do the same.

If it had been left to Frank, he would immediately have made Tony captain. However apart from having Simon to deal with, there was also John Appleton himself. As Frank had already discovered, this man was something of a barrack-room lawyer and undoubtedly a tricky customer to contemplate taking head-on at this early stage.

Frank had to keep on reminding himself that, however much there was an imperative to get on with things at Oakhill, he couldn't do everything at once. All in all though, looking back on the week, it had proved a satisfying start in several ways. Lots of things had been put in place, whereas, only seven days ago, he had been feeling almost on the point of despair. Of course it was only the tip of the iceberg compared with what needed doing longer-term.

At least he had a rather more relaxing weekend to look forward to. A bit different from spending all of it, as he had done last week, contacting players and holding protracted conversations haggling over terms and conditions. This weekend he was going to try and look at his own situation a bit more and view one or two properties in the area that Emily had been kind enough to get emailed from local estate agents. Where he was living at the moment had been convenient for a while, but it was about time he organised himself to find somewhere more suitable.

Definitely feeling it would do him good to try and take his mind off the club for at least a day or so, he tuned into the CD and sang along to his favourite Italian opera tunes on the way back home. Even the weather had turned very bright, as if a good omen for the weekend ahead. For the first time in a long while, he felt almost relaxed. He wouldn't have described his state of mind as entirely carefree, but certainly he felt in a mood to enjoy life a little more.

13

Rosie laughed in that distinctive almost theatrical-sounding way of hers and raised a glass: 'Here's to Oakhill United Football Club, its Academy and the new wonderful Executive Manager, Mr Frank Borrow, Sir!'

Dutifully, Frank raised his glass in response. They both took a deep sip and then an even deeper breath.

'Oh! That tastes good!' she exclaimed.

'It does indeed,' he responded.

'You know I must confess I had to have a quick glass of this bubbly to summon up the courage to invite you!' Again, the nervous laugh.

Somehow he couldn't bring himself to admit that he had swallowed a large glass of red wine to lend him the nerve to accept her sudden invitation. 'Sudden' as in finding a note from her through the letterbox: 'This evening: 5.30 onwards. To one or two of my Special Friends. RSVP. But make it quick!'

'You know Ben was so delighted when he got the letter saying he'd been accepted into the Academy. And he said he'd noticed you were actually watching the trials yourself. What a lift it gave him! So I felt it called for a bit of a special celebration.'

As she spoke in that polished sing-song accent that seemed to soar on the wing, almost as if delivering her lines on stage, he couldn't help but notice her expressive features became more and more lively and animated.

'And never mind Ben! I can't tell you how happy it's made me!'

They were standing in her kitchen. From facing him directly, she pirouetted round to take a quick look out towards the back of the house.

'It's such a wonderfully sunny evening as well. Do you think we should be grand and take our aperitifs outside?' And then having second thoughts: 'I'm afraid, as you can see though, it's not much of an outside. Not exactly a verandah with a panoramic view of some exotic tropical sunset, is it? But I suppose we can dream!'

Perhaps it was the verbal images she was weaving, or just the sense of intoxication from the champagne and being in her presence. But the combined effect more than cushioned him from the fact they happened to be standing in a minute garden hemmed in on all sides by gaunt-looking houses hovering over them like disapproving giants.

'Typical of me, isn't it? I love to do things on the spur of the moment! I know it's ludicrously short notice. I'm terribly afraid my other special friends aren't going to be able to come you know. Not even Ben can make it because he's out with his friends already. By the way, don't think me rude if my mobile goes and I answer it, but it'll probably be my friend Marian. Talking of Ben, I gave him some money to go out and celebrate. Getting into the Academy has already made so much of a difference to his whole personality. He brought so much GCSE homework back last night. I couldn't believe it! And he insisted on staying up till 11 o'clock to finish it.'

The mobile in her hand began to ring as if to command.

'Oh excuse me. Hello . . . oh hello Marian!'

While conversation ensued, Frank went on sipping his champagne and observing how attractive Rosie looked in an off-the-shoulder top and loose short summer skirt. Somehow, the exchange he had had with Matt Johnson sprang uncomfortably back to mind and in particular the phrase 'all fur coat and no knickers'. Well it was definitely too warm for a fur coat but . . . Reproving himself, he looked away and thought how incongruous all this was again, standing together in the back garden of a woman he barely knew, partaking of cocktails.

At last, the call came to an end. Frank gathered that Marian was unable to come.

'Oh, I feel such a fraud. It's as if I've invited you on false pretences! And I'd've so liked you to meet my one or two special friends. And them meet you of course!'

He glanced back at her non-committally. The feeling coursing through his veins was of massive relief but he wasn't going to tell her that. Perhaps he didn't need to.

'The very least I can do is offer you a top-up. Your glass is empty . . . that's with me on the phone . . . I've been neglecting my duties. Here, you hold your glass and I'll pour you another.'

Although it felt like they were playing some sort of game, Frank was quite happy to let Rosie make the running.

Another hour later and Rosie had decided she was feeling a bit hungry.

'I know a place we could go for dinner, if you're interested, that is. Oh, but am I being too forward?'

'No,' he said.

She looked back at him uncertainly.

'No you're not being too forward. Yes, I would like to go out to dinner.'

They had agreed to leave it half an hour in order to get changed. Rosie had taken it upon herself to order a taxi to take them from 3 Queen Anne's Way at 8 o'clock.

Considering how things were going, Frank was definitely feeling in a mood to enjoy life a bit more.

Frank awoke from a bad dream with sweat pouring off him. All he could recall was that he was standing on the edge of a precipice. Somehow he had toppled off and now he was in free fall to the bottom of some rocky canyon.

Wretched self-accusations had started rehearsing themselves in his head about follies perpetrated the previous evening under the influence of excessive alcohol intake. At least it was his own bed he was lying in and not anyone else's! Turning over quickly, he mouthed another prayer of gratitude to find he was there on his own.

Collecting his wits as best he could, he endeavoured to piece together again what had happened the night before. Feeling a massive sense of relief, no, nothing instantly sprang to mind to recriminate himself with. His firm recollection now was that it had been a pleasant, amicable occasion.

For some reason, a part of the evening when they were together at the dinner table came back into his head. Rosie had warmed to the theme of describing to him a holiday she'd been on in the West Indies with Ben the previous summer. She was wearing a very elegant red sleeveless dress, and he remembered in particular how she had embroidered her story with her hands and bare arms so expressively to give emphasis to what she was saying. As seemed to be the pattern, she did most of the talking while he listened and observed. And then she had suddenly taxed him: 'Are you always quite so passive?'

A little embarrassed to know how to respond, he had confessed rather too honestly, 'It's just that I like listening to you.'

At least he had kept himself from saying what he had been thinking, that he also really liked watching her as she spoke.

But, taking fuller stock this morning, he had to admit he was only being remiss if he didn't take more active note of the warning bells starting to go off in his head. At one point she had made reference to her parents. Hell, they might be younger than him! As it was anyway, he was going to need a calculator to work out the age difference between Rosie and himself.

The taxi had got them back to Queen Anne's Way by about 10.30. She had invited him in for coffee but had seen the lights on and surmised Ben was back home already. Then they had exchanged pleasantries, said goodnight and returned to their own houses.

Feeling kinder to himself in retrospect, however self-conscious about it he was, the incalculable age difference hadn't in reality felt that much of an obstacle to the two of them enjoying each other's company for a meal out. As he now pleasantly recalled, she had even said at the end, 'We must do that again some time soon.'

Just as he was smiling at this memory, his reverie was broken by the mobile going off on his bedside table. Glancing at the alarm clock, he saw it was 9.01. The wishful instinct came into his mind that he might hear Rosie on the end of the line but it was a man's voice:

'Who's been a very bad boy, then?'

Frank leapt up in bed with the same feeling of blind panic he'd had from his anxiety dream. It sounded like he was about to get a proper hauling over the coals. Even more worryingly he still couldn't recognise the voice.

Evidently, taking an attractive younger woman out to dinner was far, far more sinful than he could have dreamed of. And worse still, someone in high authority already knew of it and was about to make him suffer big-time.

'Hi there, it's Shazad!' The menacing, if rather sinister, tone suddenly changed to bright and breezy. 'How are you doing?'

'Fine, thank you,' he murmured back, his nerves all over the place.

'Yes! Naughty boys get their knuckles rapped for doing bad things like signing up new players you know?'

Oh thank goodness for that! Somehow Frank could also detect that Shazad seemed himself to be taking things with a considerable pinch of salt.

Then the other man went off in satirical vein. 'Yes our Chairman is very indignant about it. Angry even, I suspect. It's needled him into sending an agenda out in advance of our next Board meeting. That's another first in the history of Oakhill United FC!'

Frank listened with fresh interest to judge where all this might be going.

'Yes, the number one item is "FB's Roles and Responsibilities".

Unofficially, I can tell you the chair has circulated photocopies of the back page of *The Oakhill Times* article on the signing of those two players. He has also attached a note saying how incumbent it is on the Board to question the procedures and even . . . I quote, "The validity of those two transfers".'

Despite the obvious way in which Shazad was suggesting the Chair was over-reacting, Frank still felt somewhat concerned. Having thought he was doing the club a favour by signing up Bennison and Carpenter, he could see that others, especially the Chair, might not be prepared to see it in that light at all. Where that left him, he couldn't quite be sure.

'I can tell you, Frank, that I'll be one hundred per cent behind you at the meeting. We desperately need good players and we have to back your judgement. That's the top and bottom of it for me! By the way, you know I was talking to you about a group of us businessmen putting together a consortium take-over bid? I can tell you we're well on our way to doing that and I intend presenting the bid to the Board at this next meeting. Do I take it you'll give us your backing?'

As well-disposed as Frank felt to Shazad, he wasn't intending to be steam-rollered. 'I think I'd need to see the bid first,' he made clear.

'Of course . . . of course! We want you to be involved with us in hammering it out in its final form. But in principle?'

'Yes, in principle, I'm behind you.'

'That's excellent to hear, Frank.'

Reeling from the thought of the boardroom battle ahead, with himself likely to be the whipping boy in the middle of it all, Frank suddenly felt like bringing the conversation to a stop at this point.

'Just one more thing, Frank! I was really pleased to be contacted by two guys called Khan and Mahmood who were delighted their sons had been taken on in the Academy. It was another thing we were talking about last time we met, if you remember?'

Oh yes, Frank remembered all right! But he had honestly

been impressed by the strength and ability of the lads in question.

As their chat finally came to an end, Frank felt he could take comfort from the fact his close interest in the Academy trials had ended up pleasing more than just one parent. However, he sincerely hoped the others wouldn't get carried away and invite him to join them in celebrations too. When all was said and done, there was really only one parent he felt he would enjoy that kind of occasion in the company of.

It was 6 o'clock on the Sunday by the time Frank had got back home from his last viewing. With her usual thoroughness, Emily had mapped out a programme of house visits which was well organised and carefully thought through. He had gone to look around six properties in all, three yesterday and the remaining three today, all within a 15-mile radius of the club. He had been happy enough to leave the short-listing down to Emily. In the event, he couldn't say any of them were unattractive houses, which said as much about his PA's good taste as the properties themselves. But none of them, in his present state of mind, had really grabbed him. And as he thought how he would put it to Emily, he knew he was going to find it difficult to come up with a reasonable explanation. Perhaps it was just that his heart hadn't felt as fully engaged in the search for a new place as it needed to be. On returning home, something still seemed to be holding him back, as if to say there wasn't a tearing hurry yet to find anywhere else.

As the evening wore on, thoughts of the week ahead at Oakhill United started to teem back into his head. One decision he needed to ponder was how quickly to seek to implement his plan to replace John Appleton as captain with Tony Bennison. That whole question had begun to preoccupy his mind even more strongly than on Friday. Those same issues as had been taxing him at the end of the week, were still crying out to be resolved. But then, based on his conversation with Shazad, it now appeared his quick-fire signings of Bennison and Carpenter were set to spark broader controversy.

It was beginning to look as if he needed to commit himself from the start to backing Tony Bennison to the hilt. If he could offload Appleton somewhere else at the same time, that would serve a double benefit because it would mean the club had to pay one less set of wages. Even if Frank couldn't effect a transfer, it might be possible to make a loan arrangement. After all, lots of clubs were still in the market and clamouring to find new players at the last minute. It was difficult to say for sure whether Appleton himself would be willing to play ball. He was going to have to see.

Thinking of the two new players he'd brought with him from his old club, he appreciated it was likely to be as difficult for them adapting as it had been for himself. In their case, it might be even more difficult, from being 'tagged' as Frank's players. Although no blatant hostility had been shown them, there were always subtle ways in which a new player could be made to feel unwelcome. For example, in Tony's case, Frank couldn't help but notice how in training, if both Tony and John Appleton shouted for the ball to be passed to them, other players unfailingly deferred to the club captain and starved the 'new boy' of possession. Perhaps these were just old-established habits but for a player like Tony, with his far greater ability, it was likely to prove extremely frustrating not to say downright annoying. Besides, if this practice extended to matches, it was going to be fatal as far as team results were concerned. These were matters Frank was all too well aware he was going to have to get to grips with during the coming week. But at least, he could console himself, it didn't feel like his head was quite so spinning this week with things he needed to tackle head-on.

Switching off the lights on the two lower floors and climbing the stairs up to his bedroom, a curious idea entered his head. Was the person living at 3 Queen's Way, with its identical build to his house, right now doing exactly the same thing? Then, upon entering his bedroom, for some strange reason again his thoughts veered back to the conversation he had had with Matt Johnson. If it were true that Rosie Skipton had had an affair with Matt's predecessor Andy, previous occupant of 8 Queen's Way, she might well have slept in the same bed he was about to climb into.

Trying to shut dangerous images out of mind, he accepted it was better he got his head properly back on football matters in readiness for the following day.

14

Emily stared critically yet again at herself in the mirror and wondered. Darting a glance at her watch, she noted it was only 7.30. It certainly wasn't too late to change back out of the sharp new black trouser suit she'd bought over the weekend. And if she did that, she wouldn't have to worry either about potential reaction to the new pair of patent leather shoes she was wearing which had heels a good two inches higher than she had ever been seen in before. Surely the whole look erred far too much on the showy side? Or, hang on a moment, didn't some new, daring instinct tell her just to go for it?

With a braveness of spirit that surprised even herself, she had determined it was make-or-break time. Anyway, after all the effort she'd put in over the weekend to revitalise her appearance, it would be plain copping out to revert to going into work as usual in one of her long line of comfortable outfits with horribly sensible shoes to match. It had been particularly confidence-enhancing to recall just how enthusiastic the assistant had been about saying Emily had the perfect figure for the trouser suit. She had felt invigorated. In another store she had gone on a veritable spree buying summer tops, skirts and new undies. She had also had her hair cut and coloured a darker brown tone to zap that growing edge of grey. Then she had had her nails manicured, even if in the end she'd settled for a more subtle silver than the brash red she had been originally tempted by. Although she had been nervous about submitting herself to a so-called 'make-over', she had finally snapped and gone for it. Suffering the perpetual state of anxiety in approaching forty, doing something about her appearance was a bridge she had to cross before it was too late.

Nor did she believe she could afford to go on being timid in other directions. True, she had managed to summon up the nerve, or whatever it was, to commit herself to entering her details on the soulmate website. But she had soon come to realise it had only been scratching the surface compared with what she was actually searching for in the way of personal fulfilment. As she had thought so often recently, dear Martin was sweet and pleasant-natured in his own way, but she had to face up to the fact she was really hoping for, or even dying for, a deeper relationship which would prove satisfying in other ways besides. The stark alternative was a haunting vision of the future in which she was marooned as a sad old spinster in a bedsit. God, she had to do something and do it quick!

So apart from dedicating the larger part of her weekend to unashamedly tarting up her appearance, she had decided to dissect her existing soulmate description of herself. Not to put too fine a point on it, she needed to convey herself as an altogether more exciting person. Otherwise, the only men she would ever meet would be clones of Martin! In her original desire to sound at all costs tasteful, she had completely sacrificed any oomph factor. No wonder then, at the very best, she now seemed doomed to a diet of the type of cultural engagements that entertained but failed to satisfy her.

The only trouble was that for all the time she had spent over the weekend playing around with her pen-portrait, she hadn't yet been able to come up with anything approaching a suitable formula of words. Terms like 'fun-loving' seemed merely to be token vapidity. Perhaps it might aid self-promotion to describe herself as 'gregarious' but actually she wasn't. Did she have a passionate side? She knew she did but, however much of a more exciting life she was hankering after, over her dead body was she prepared to put a line like that on record. Reluctantly, she decided she would have to put the editing process to one side for the time being.

Apprehensive inside as to how people at work were going to react to her new image, in the event she couldn't help observing quite a few heads turning in her direction. Even Simon Steele noticed and paid her a compliment. Jack Hubbard appeared positively arrested in mid-stride. As if suffering from a sudden bout of amnesia, he seemed totally at a loss to recall the usual range of TV programmes he was accustomed to analysing on her behalf. As for Frank Borrow, she sadly reflected he had only glanced once in passing when handing her something he needed photocopying. He might as well have been looking at the photocopier itself.

'It's obvious you want to get rid of me! Don't you?'

John Appleton sat bolt upright in the chair opposite him with what could only be described as a glower on his face.

'No, it's not like that at all John,' Frank said, uncomfortably aware he was lying through his teeth. 'It's just that a player like yourself who's been at the one club so long should be looking to broaden their experience.'

'But I told you when we first met, I like it here.' The look on the other man's face changed to a curious blend of obstinacy and self-righteousness. 'I've been a loyal servant to Oakhill United and this is how I get treated!'

'It's not like that, John,' Frank repeated, realising he would need to take it up a gear or two if he were to get his message across effectively. 'I've been round enough clubs myself to know that you have to keep extending options available to you. No offence, but you're not exactly in your prime as a player, are you?'

John's mouth twitched involuntarily as if he could have said something in immediate response but thought better of it. He just sat there glumly. Not wishing the other man to descend into despondency, Frank smiled in a vain effort to coax some similar reaction back, but had to admit defeat. Instead, overdrive seemed the only mode. 'What I was going to say was that I could find you a new club . . . one where they'd be prepared to pay you over and above what you're earning now to do some coaching as well as going on playing.'

Frank noticed John's features crack ever so gradually, first a slight puckering of the brow in surprise and then an unmistakable glint of interest in the eye.

'Would that be at a club within travelling distance? Because I'm used to this area and wouldn't want to have to up sticks.'

Oh my word! The tactic was beginning to work. 'I actually know just the place,' Frank said with a manufactured tone of authority in his voice.

'Where is it?' the other man pressed.

'I'm not at liberty to say yet for obvious reasons, but I felt I had a duty to check it out with you first to see if you might be interested.'

'Oh yes, I might be interested in it, I suppose.'

Although he tried to curb his enthusiasm with the 'I suppose', Frank could tell he was definitely warming to the bait.

'By the way, does the gaffer know about any of this?' John pursued.

Frank assumed he meant Simon Steele. 'Er . . . yes,' he replied hesitantly. 'But he thought I should be the one to put the option to you.'

That was indeed true. What he didn't add was that Simon had virtually jumped up and down at the possibility of losing the club captain who, by his own admission, had been an utter thorn in his side since coming to the club.

'What does the gaffer think, then?'

Frank paused a moment or two, swallowing hard on what best to say in response.

'He too would be sorry to see you go but doesn't want to stand in the way of your future professional development.'

The thought occurred to Frank he had better clarify for sure any outstanding contractual issues before making serious contact with one or two other clubs he had in mind.

'It's my understanding that you still have two years left on your present contract. Is that right?'

'Yes.'

Frank tried to put out of mind the club's self-evident stupidity in having granted Appleton a longer-term contract whereas quality players like Brown, Marrison and Pierce had been lost by only being given meagre one-year terms of employment.

'What I would be thinking of was at the very least seeing if a one-year loan arrangement couldn't be secured at another club. Of course that would give you the discretion to decide what you wanted to do at the end of that year. It could mean you coming back here to complete the second year of your contract. But it would still leave you with the option.'

Although it sounded like he was weakening a bit, he had to reserve himself the widest room for manoeuvre in striking a deal. Besides, which club in its right mind would want to sign Appleton outright?

'That sounds fine by me,' came back the gratifying response.

By the end of the meeting it had felt like John Appleton was well up for the move. 'When do you think you might know, boss?' had been his last anxious-sounding plea.

'I'll get back to you within the next twenty-four hours.'

As soon as John had closed the door behind him, Frank set himself frantically to ring round with the express aim of drawing in favours from would-be contacts. First port of call was a protégé of his, Colin Turner, an ex-player from one of his former clubs who he'd encouraged to apply successfully to become manager of a team by chance only twenty miles down the road from Oakhill. By another strange coincidence, Frank had read in the papers that he had very recently lost two of his key midfielders with serious, long-term injuries. Like lightning he was on the phone advocating strongly to Colin to consider taking on Appleton to cover the obvious crisis.

Not to put too fine a point on things, Frank had learnt the hard way himself that, to stay in the game, a manager had to be adept in wheeling and dealing. How else could you survive without committing the occasional devious act to keep head above the water? But it wasn't as if he hadn't done Colin genuinely good turns in the past. It could even be argued, in present circumstances, he was doing him yet another good turn by offering the services of his experienced club captain, John Appleton, in the face of an apparent emergency.

Whatever the reality of the matter, it couldn't help but serve a useful purpose from his own point of view, in going the extra mile to get this unwanted player out of Oakhill's hair. Then at least he could proceed with making Tony captain in his place. Of course, he needed for appearances' sake to square all this with Simon, but from his demeanour so far, Frank didn't anticipate any trouble from that direction.

Despite everything, Frank couldn't stop himself enjoying a quiet chuckle all day as he thought back to the slightly Machiavellian way that business had been transacted.

Frank had started the day as he meant to go on. That was even before his meeting with John Appleton. For the first time that morning, he had actually succeeded in arriving in the club car park before Simon Steele. Just as a prank, he had parked his car in the space reserved for 'The Manager'. He hadn't been out to make any particular point, let alone intending to usurp the spot longer-term, but had to admit to being curious as to how the other man might react. Within half an hour, Frank was amused to see that an email had been circulated by the site manager requiring the owner of a car with a certain registration number to remove it from the said space. But because Frank was already busy with much else, he didn't react instantly.

OK, so he was in slightly mischievous mode. But despite the pending Board meeting lingering in the back of his mind, he was still determined to press on with player transactions and just report these to the Board when the time arose. If he was in trouble already over Bennison and Carpenter, he may as well be hung for a sheep as a lamb!

With the Appleton business now in full swing, Frank was sitting back in his office allowing his eye to run down the rest of the squad-list to remind himself of other expendable players. Pausing for a moment to switch his mobile back on after the meeting, his spirits felt exhilarated to see there was a text message stored in his inbox from none other than Rosie Skipton. They had exchanged numbers on the Friday night. For whatever reason, he had resisted contacting her over the weekend but then had felt unjustifiably disappointed when he hadn't received one himself. The message read:

> *Really enjoyed Friday. How about coming Friday evening?*
> *My turn to pay!*

Frank didn't need to look in any diary to know he was available.

Suddenly, everything felt sunshine and roses. But he would have to watch himself a bit. It was bad enough that he was already quietly chuckling to himself over the cheek of the Appleton business. Now, as he looked at his face in the mirror, he caught an almost gaga image beaming back at him. An impulse told him not to dwell in his office but instead get himself out and about. But don't look quite so chuffed. Still feeling in a highly congenial frame of mind, the first thing he did was go and remove his car from Simon's reserved bay.

'Didn't bother me at all! Thought it quite funny. Only the site manager is a stickler for things like that. He didn't realise it was your car,' Simon had responded.

Frank was feeling light-hearted enough to want to do something else he'd been dying to do since starting at the club. Why not? Following up on the precedent of arriving first and taking the other man's parking space, he now aimed a playful punch into Simon's solar plexus straight between the two Ss on his tracksuit.

'You're a good man, Simon!' he said in a tone of voice spiced with team-building bonhomie.

119

'You're not trying to tell me something, are you?' Simon offered back gamely, no doubt wondering what the other man was on today.

An appropriate opportunity for bringing Frank back down to earth must have been running through Simon's mind though. After quietly digesting his update on the Appleton loan arrangement, he waited for a few seconds and then lifted up an envelope from his desk. Frank could see it was already opened.

'It was addressed to me . . . from a lot of the players. I think a copy's been sent to the Chair as well.'

'Oh, what is it? The threat of a walk-out on the basis of things that have happened since I joined the club?'

The other man looked back at him as if he possessed supernatural powers.

'Well, bring it on is what I say!' Frank's voice rang out defiantly.

Emily couldn't help but notice that the whole club seemed to be in a state of seething discontent. The only person who acted as if he were totally oblivious to it all was Frank Borrow. At least it wasn't just her make-over that he appeared not to have noticed today.

With regard to the general situation, she couldn't quite be sure whether it was down to sheer, strong-willed determination on his part or simply that he was blissfully unaware. Or perhaps it was even his way of forcing an actual showdown with those players he thought were obviously not pulling their weight.

But whichever way, she didn't like to think he might allow himself to become too unpopular. Apart from the two players he had recently signed, there didn't seem too much love lost between Frank and anyone else. She would have hated Frank to think she was feeling sorry for him but, not least as PA, she thought she should take it upon herself to make a special effort to look after him. Unfortunately though, it seemed there was little else she could do beyond going into his office and asking whether he would like her to make another cup of coffee.

Two or three times in the early afternoon she had made the offer but he had declined each time. Then, at around 4 o'clock, she had popped her head round the door and said cheerily, 'I'm making a brew. Do you fancy one?'

'Go on then!' he had relented.

About to go and do the necessary, she heard him call her back. 'By the way, I didn't like to say but . . .' She waited for him to finish the sentence but he suddenly became hesitant. It was as if he had had something very definite to say but it had clean gone out of his mind . . . some kind of senior moment.

For a while she even thought he might be about to report back on the houses on his visiting list over the weekend. Instead, as if having to summon up courage, he had expressed himself in a convincing tone: 'By the way I was about to say . . . only I didn't, in case it offended . . . but I think you look sensational today. In fact you look a million dollars, if you don't mind me saying so.'

Offended? That was the last thing she felt.

'Well thank you very much,' she merely offered in return, not quite knowing what to say.

With his eyes maintaining a level gaze, it almost felt as though some explanation might be required of her as to how she had achieved such an obvious transformation. But all she ended up saying was, 'I'll go and make the coffee then.'

'Yes,' he said, abruptly returning to study some papers on his desk.

When Emily got back home that evening, she instantly took out her pen portrait again and indulged herself in playing around with the phrases 'looks really sensational' and 'looks a million dollars'. She probably couldn't use these words but the fact Frank had spoken them made her feel unbelievably happy about herself.

15

Frank had found it odd he hadn't received any official invitation to the Board meeting or even notification of what was on the agenda. Given his conversation with Shazad, he had thought about getting in touch with Arnold Preston himself but had wanted to have another chat with Shazad before doing so. As well as his various dealings with players, not to mention the complaint about him that had been submitted to the Chair from the so-called 'backbone' of the team, there was also of course the potential matter of the consortium bid. He had tried contacting Shazad throughout the forty-eight hours leading up to the meeting on the Wednesday for an update on how the bid was progressing, but had drawn a blank. Frank had left three messages but there had been no response. For a businessman who seemed to pride himself on being as sharp as a tack, it felt a bit disconcerting.

He had casually raised the topic of Board meetings in general with Simon Steele who had instantaneously responded with that threatened look of a tomcat sensing a territory invasion. Clearly Simon was likely to be taking the view, on the basis of precedent, that it was his sole right to attend such meetings as the manager appointed by the Board. When Frank chose not to press the subject, Simon relented with a shrug of his shoulders and expressed the view that attending such meetings was a wearisome chore and that he was envious of Frank that he didn't have to waste his time attending them.

I'll be the judge of that, Frank quietly thought to himself. In the event, although he held off making a decision whether to attend the meeting or not until the night itself, he had ultimately taken it upon himself to gatecrash the party.

Short of having bouncers standing on the door, the reaction of others to his arrival was as welcoming as a wet weekend. At the top of the table, the two spaces were occupied by the Chair and Simon Steele sitting shoulder to shoulder studying some document or other. Both men momentarily lifted their eyes as if with a synchronised flicker of irritation at the fact he had presumed to butt in on their proceedings. With a couple of minutes to go to the starting-time, other board-members were circled round an urn drinking cups of tea. But no sign of Shazad. Not having met any of them before, except for Jed who Frank knew was the players' representative on the Board, he decided just to sit down quietly and interest himself in some notes he had brought with him on the squad list. Out of the corner of his eye, he caught Jed giving him an old-fashioned stare.

'Well, shall we make a start, gentlemen?' Arnold called out. Frank wryly observed how quickly and obediently the others all took to their seats.

'There's quite a lot of business to get through,' the Chair paused and then, looking over the top of his reading glasses in the style of a presiding member of the judiciary, 'and this is even before the season's new fixture list has commenced.'

A little peal of appreciative laughter broke out around the table, giving Frank a disquieting reminder of Arnold Preston's presentational dexterity.

'Can I turn to Item One which is Playing Staff for the new season?'

Frank made a mental note that the agenda item wasn't quite billed in the same way as Shazad had led him to believe. Either it had been adapted since or else it had been a wind-up on Shazad's part. One way and another he was beginning to feel rather stupid believing anything Shazad said to him.

'Simon, I'm turning to you as our manager for this item, although I would like Board members to note that we are unexpectedly graced also with the presence of the Executive Manager on this occasion.'

Heads turned in Frank's direction although more out of curiosity than politeness. Without a hint of a welcoming smile, faces switched back to paying rapt attention to the Chair.

'Well, we've lost Brown, Marrison, and Pierce over the close season,' Simon started out. 'But I have to say we were semi-expecting they would go because they were on one-year contracts.'

Everyone round the table nodded as if it was unavoidable the three of them having left the club.

'Any new players?' the Chair prompted in an innocent-sounding tone.

The manager hesitated as if reluctant to comment. Frank noticed how Simon snatched a shifty look in his own direction but said nothing.

'I only ask,' the Chair took up, 'because presumably no doubt like other members of the Board, I happened to be informed of the signing of two new players from reading the story on the back page of *The Oakhill Times* . . .'

As a matter of habit, Emily always bought herself a copy of *The Oakhill Times* on a Wednesday evening. That was the edition during the week that concentrated most strongly on job adverts. Having said that, the exercise had proved fruitless to this point. There had been remarkably few jobs of interest to her advertised in recent weeks. Tonight though, she had spotted something that leapt off the page. The position in question was a Senior Business Systems Analyst/Project Manager working in the local council's Chief Executive's Department, at £40k+. The box advert was a replica of the post Emily had carried out in London. Reading the job specification it seemed an almost complete match of skills required:

- *The ability to capture and analyse complex problems . . .*
- *Developing high level system requirements . . .*
- *Advanced organisational and communication skills . . .*

Now, plus the fact she had taken the necessary steps over the weekend to succeed in making herself 'look a million dollars' with her new image, what could possibly stop her?

From very first sight of the advert she felt a strong urge to apply and had immediately emailed for the application form. Already, in her mind's eye, she had decided to put Frank Borrow down as one of her referees. She would of course have to check with him that he would be willing to support her application.

It was beyond 9 o'clock now. The Board meeting had lasted more than two hours by the time Arnold Preston brought himself to summarise the way forward for the Board to address a number of the agenda items that had been discussed.

'On the playing staff side, it is noted that we have lost three players from last year's squad and gained two new players for the season ahead. Although the Executive Manager has put forward a case for the need to draft in new players, the Board feels it has no alternative but to censure the methods by which these two new existing signings have been made clearly in contravention of the Board's regulations.'

Sounding rather like a hanging judge exercising a degree of clemency in the particular circumstances of the case, the Chair continued with his summing-up.

'Because the Executive Manager is new to the club, it is appreciated therefore that he may have not been as fully aware of the protocols as he would have been otherwise. No blame whatsoever, though, in this respect should be attributed to the Board's appointed manager Simon Steele, who we accept was unaware of these signings until such time as the players in question were introduced to him on the Monday. While, on balance, it has been decided no action will be taken to seek to nullify these particular transfers, management is both warned and duly notified that it is obliged to follow the Board's laid-down procedures on a satisfactory basis in future.'

Barely pausing, the Chair breathlessly continued, almost as if there had been a televised game Board members were dying to get back home to. 'Next, we have been notified by the auditors that the club will be in receipt of their report findings, with accompanying recommendations, within the next week. For you as Board members, I give my assurance that you will have a copy of the full report in your hands within twenty-four hours of its submission by the auditing firm. It is vitally important that this matter is an item on our next Board meeting agenda in two weeks' time. Thirdly, it is my duty to remind you as Board members that, as Chair, I notified you I had received a letter of complaint from certain of the more senior players about many of the changes that have taken place at the club since the recent arrival of the new Executive Manager. It has been decided that a sub-committee of three Board members should investigate the complaints with a view hopefully to seeking to resolve any difficulties that may have inadvertently or otherwise sprung up. It is of paramount importance, in my view, that Oakhill United, which has always been a happy club, is given full chance to continue as such in future.'

Finishing on that note, Arnold then took the step of looking carefully around the table to satisfy himself he had the Board's backing in everything he had put forward on their behalf. His glance was met with nods of approval.

Meanwhile, Frank himself was seething at the way in which matters had been handled. Ruefully, he wondered how he would have felt if such outcomes had been reached in his absence. At least, by being there, he had been able to present the case for measures he had taken since arriving at Oakhill, for example beefing up training schedules to commit players to better levels of match preparation.

'Can I ask if there is any other business?' The Chair sought to wrap up proceedings.

This was the part of the meeting, Frank had cause to reflect, at which Shazad had given him to believe he would be raising the matter of the consortium take-over bid. But of course the person in question was still conspicuous by his absence.

'In that case, if there is no other business, I thank you for your attendance, gentlemen, and thereby declare the meeting closed,' the Chair concluded.

Frank didn't feel persuaded to stay in the room one moment longer than he needed to and departed instantly. It went without saying he couldn't help but feel badly let down by how matters had proceeded at this Board meeting. Not to put too fine a point on things he would have hoped for much stronger support from both the Chair and the Board as a whole. To whatever extent he had conducted himself in restrained fashion during the meeting, certainly not wishing to engage in any confrontation, Frank did not feel in a mood to take things lying down in future.

The next morning at work, Frank had made it his priority to hold a solid hour-long meeting with Simon. Definitely, the purpose behind this was not to vent his spleen about the Board meeting. That would have been a complete waste of time. Anyway, Simon would just have listened and then faithfully relayed Frank's comments word for word to Arnold Preston.

Instead, Frank's intention was to get to grips with team selection and tactics for the opening game of the season this coming Saturday. Although naturally there had been some discussion of such matters already during the last couple of weeks, Frank's take on it was that nothing had yet been agreed upon, let alone finalised. On his way to work, worst scenario, he had visualised himself raising the matter only for Simon to reply stroppily, 'I've already picked the team. If you want to see what it is, the sheet is pinned up on the players' noticeboard.'

If it had in fact happened like that, Frank had predetermined he would come back with some pithy response like: 'You can go back to that noticeboard, take the list down and rip it to pieces. Should you not wish to do that, I damn well will!' Was he becoming paranoid?

Thankfully, if only to preserve the colour of the air in Simon's office from turning royal blue, a different kind of response was forthcoming from the man in question: 'I was waiting for you to raise the matter and then hoping we could discuss it between us.'

Perhaps the lad's learning after all, Frank thought. Even if nowhere nearly as quickly as he needed to.

'Well, how about this?' Frank put to him, looking to capitalise on the other man's mood of cooperation.

'Yes, go on. I'd be surprised if we're not pretty well in agreement.'

How promising did that sound?

'OK then. Harris in goal of course. Price and Farmer centre-back.'

'In total agreement,' Simon affirmed.

'Can't see how we have any option for the moment but to keep playing Jed Forrester at right-back although you know my reservations: slower than the average thirty-year-old carthorse!'

The throwaway remark at least succeeded in eliciting a grudging smile from Simon who took it upon himself to offer back, 'Not sure whether you know this but Jed picked up a League 2 record last year.'

Frank sensed he was about to be granted a rare treat: a helpful disclosure of information from Simon.

'Yes, Jed achieved the highest combined number of yellow and red cards ever picked up in one season in League 2. Not sure I'd be proud of it myself, but it's a bit of a claim to fame for our Jed.'

'Some achievement, isn't it?' Frank replied. Thinking back to the previous evening, Jed wasn't exactly his favourite player at the moment for all kinds of reasons. He was a leading member of the notorious 'backbone' brigade, and Frank was already bent on getting rid of this painfully slow full-back. Apart from anything else, he seemed to be also setting himself up to become Appleton's replacement as team barrack-room lawyer.

'With Trenton defending as full-back on the left . . .'

Simon nodded. 'Yes that lad's come on terrific . . . especially with the new training regime. He's positively lapped it up.'

Frank was beginning to find it almost disconcerting how eye-to-eye he and Simon appeared to be getting on this morning. Or perhaps the other man must have been thinking to himself he owed Frank one hell of a lot of cosying up to, on account of last night's Board meeting.

'I would go for a 4-5-1 formation,' Frank pressed on, 'with Carpenter playing the out-and-out striker role and Bennison breaking from midfield to support as and when possible. That leaves four more across midfield consisting of Wilson, Riley, Bolland and Shenanigan.'

Frank reckoned he had better extend some humour back in Simon's direction with the intended mispronunciation of the left-winger, whose real name was Shanahan.

Ignoring the play on words, Simon kept his mind on practicalities. 'Now Appleton's gone, the team kind of picks itself, doesn't it?'

Frank looked to consolidate. 'We're in agreement then?'

'Reckon so.'

'Do you think we should break the news this morning? Then discuss the 4-5-1 tactic during the team talk?'

'OK by me.'

Frank might still feel unable to trust Simon in other more 'political' matters but in terms of basic team selection, they seemed to have a more common perception of things. Good heavens, Frank thought to himself, they had agreed on something!

16

'Look I couldn't blame you for writing me off as a complete jerk. Not for one moment, I couldn't.'

It was Shazad Ali on the line. Frank certainly couldn't quibble with this opening statement. Still, it was one thing admitting he had failed to do what he had said he was going to do. Quite another to provide any satisfactory explanation as to why. Frank did not feel appeased in the least. In truth, going on pouring scorn and criticism on himself wasn't what Frank either needed or wanted to hear. It was beginning to sound like ritualistic self-indulgence. Vainly, he went on waiting for any attempt at justi-fication for what appeared on the face of it a total foul-up, not returning any of Frank's calls and then failing to make it to the Board meeting.

'I know you'd be perfectly within your rights not to trust my word ever again.'

Frank was tiring rapidly of this. He was determined not to commit himself to saying anything until Shazad made a state-ment that actually contained something substantial enough for him to respond to. But there was a limit to how long he could go on listening and he finally snapped. 'So are you in effect saying the consortium bid is a complete non-starter now?'

There was a silence on the other end of the line as if Shazad was nonplussed by Frank's rasping candour.

'No, I'm definitely not saying that.'

'Well what exactly are you saying?'

'I'm saying . . . I'm saying . . .' Oh no, the hesitation made it sound like he was biding his time again before coming up with more empty wordmongering. 'I'm saying I let you down because I didn't get back in touch with you before the meeting.'

Well at least he was big enough to admit that.

'But then you didn't even make it to the meeting itself!' Frank rammed the point home.

'I can explain that.'

'Please do, I really would appreciate hearing an explanation!'

To Frank, all this seemed to be going round in circles.

'I actually rang the Chair of the Board to ask when the Auditors' Report would be out and he said it wouldn't be out until a week later. Knowing our consortium was writing a bid, I made the decision not to attend any Board meetings until the Auditors' Report was properly out on the table. Nor, in the end, did I think it was a good idea to give the Board any prior warning of our bid at this stage.'

'So why didn't you contact me to say this, then?'

'Because I only managed to make contact with Arnold Preston an hour or two before the meeting. I hadn't intended ringing you of course until I'd spoken to the Chair. In the event, I fully apologise for not managing to get back to you.'

The charitable side of Frank thought the explanation sounded just about plausible. The less accommodating side of him found it much too convenient for comfort. But in any case, the meeting had gone now. Painful as it seemed, he owed it to himself to get a take on where matters stood for the next meeting.

'Believe me, Frank, our bid will be on the table. The Auditors' Report will be out and no good is going to come of it. The club will not be able to survive in its present form. Our consortium will take over and we need your support.'

How quickly, Frank thought, Shazad had got himself back into the messiah mode once again, courting disciples to his cause. Why, only minutes earlier, he had conceded that Frank would be perfectly within his rights not to trust his word ever again.

Was there anything about this new, latest pledge, that warranted

Frank having confidence in it? Up to this point, none whatsoever.

Probably the only reason why he was prepared to go on placing any degree of trust in what Shazad had to say was that, by comparison, Frank had even less reason to trust Arnold Preston. The other main trouble was that even if the consortium managed to get its act together and put its bid forward, there was no guarantee of it being accepted. But whatever else did or didn't happen in the meantime, Frank was determined not to find himself waltzing into another Board meeting without knowing the full score.

On the Friday morning when Frank went into work, Simon almost accosted him, ushering him straight into his office.

'The Chairman was on the phone to me last night,' he announced with an anxious look on his face. Frank thought, how could Simon know for sure the Chair hadn't spoken to him also? OK, he had to admit, it was a daft question even to put to himself. Not least because the Chair hadn't contacted him on one single occasion since he'd started. In suspense to hear what it was about, he sincerely hoped the Chair hadn't caught wind of the pending consortium bid.

'The Chair has received a preliminary copy of the final Auditors' Report and it doesn't look good. In fact, far worse than anyone might have thought.'

Although Frank took it upon himself to assume a pained, sympathetic expression on his face, he had to confess to himself that it sounded rather good news. It was long overdue that the club got its wake-up call.

'Yes the outcome is that certain measures have to be taken with immediate effect.' As he said this, Simon seemed to be staring straight past him and in the general direction of Jack Hubbard's office. Frank divined this couldn't be completely coincidental.

Meanwhile, bit between teeth, Simon continued. 'We knew the club was facing problems. Only it seems now that much more

serious irregularities have been uncovered. The Chair, you understand, isn't yet of course at liberty to say publicly what it all
amounts to. But it's clear everything's going to come out in the
wash.'

It felt a little ironic to Frank to hear the rookie expressing
himself like the seasoned campaigner, but he somehow found it
within him to hold back.

'Immediate upshot is,' Simon saw fit to continue, 'that Jack
Hubbard has been suspended pending further investigation of
financial processes. He's been told not to come into the office
today and to clear his desk over the weekend.'

As if he were still keeping something even more serious up his
sleeve, Simon then decided to impart, 'From the Auditors' Report,
it looks like the club's in debt to the tune of at least two million
pounds!'

Despite the young man's total inexperience in relation to matters
concerning club finances, Frank still could not see how any of
this should come as a complete surprise to Simon.

'The Chair told me to pass on to you to keep matters quiet
for the time being until the Auditors' Report comes out officially.'

Of course. However tempting it was to get in touch with Shazad
Ali again, he was minded to resist the impulse. For the time being
at least.

Emily had been nervous about going in and seeing Frank to ask
for a reference. Apart from anything else, he had looked very
preoccupied during the last couple of days. That was perhaps
putting it a bit mildly. She had witnessed him in a terrible mood
on the Wednesday morning after the Board meeting.

That morning, she recalled, she only asked him how the meeting
had gone and he had snapped her head off. He had then ranted
on mysteriously about 'people you can trust and people you can't'
before going on alarmingly to state that 'with or without a paddle,
this whole club is completely up the creek!' It reminded her faintly
of how he had reacted after the interview with the local reporter.

Only then, eventually, there had been a twinkle in his eye to reassure her he was capable of keeping things in proportion. This time round, though, any such acknowledgement was not forthcoming. Although she hadn't taken any of it personally, she had felt powerless to know what she might say to improve his mood.

It certainly hadn't seemed an appropriate time to raise the question of her job application. At least, though, she could derive consolation from knowing when it was best just to offer him a coffee and then make a run for it.

Whatever had gone on at the Board meeting, it didn't need any sixth sense to understand the added pressure there was on him with the first match of the season looming up on Saturday. With it being a home game, there was an extra buzz of excitement around the place that seemed to be pulling at everyone's nerve ends. While she appreciated it was all new to her, she couldn't help pick up a growing sense of panic among all these 'football people' including of course the players. Having presumably gone through the experience countless times before, she would have expected them to be a little calmer. But as she often had cause to reflect, despite it all boiling down to kicking a ball around, they tended to take it very seriously. For the good of the club and people's continued livelihood, she just wished they were rather better at it than seemed to be the case.

For a while though, she thought Frank had become a bit calmer after he had had the meeting with Simon to sort out team matters. They had apparently picked the side to play on the Saturday and spent a lot of time that day and the next working with the team on tactics. The most enduring image had been seeing Frank standing in playing kit in his office on the Thursday morning waiting anxiously for the day to start. Seeing him pacing up and down, she had tried to rid herself of the thought running through her head that, by any standards, he had a pretty good pair of legs. Again though, she had somehow decided it wasn't the right time to ask for a reference.

But it was now Friday and she felt she had to broach the matter with him. If only because the last thing she wanted was for someone from the council offices to make contact and then for him to think she had lacked the professional courtesy to mention it. She had tried to speak to him first thing but Simon had grabbed him, as if both men's lives depended on it, for one of those long meetings they seemed to have got into the habit of holding together over recent days. She couldn't really tell whether these meetings were a sign of them getting on better or just another indication of the state of tension that was building up all the time towards Saturday.

Eventually, when Frank had emerged from Simon's office, she tried as nicely as possible to intercept him before he went out for another lengthy session with the players.

'Do you mind if I catch you for a brief moment?' she asked. Knowing the driven mood he was in, she was even prepared for him telling her to get lost. To think she had once thought of him as measured and tranquil of manner!

'So long as you've got a safe pair of hands,' he said with a facetiousness that was anything but settling.

On entering his office, she felt more than a little nervous in addressing him almost formally. 'I've applied for a full-time post in the Chief Executive's office of the local council. It's a kind of Business Manager post but I wondered if you would be willing to act as a referee?'

With his eyes slightly averted as he listened her out, he came back instantly with, 'Do I need to bring a whistle then?'

Oh my god, she had definitely picked a wrong time, hadn't she? He didn't look pleased to have to give it a second's consideration.

Then she heard him apologise with a slightly nervous grin. 'Forgive me. Think things are getting to me. Of course I'll give you a reference but I really do need to talk to you, Emily.'

He looked at her as if he were about to say something else but changed his mind. After another pause, he added, 'Is there some interview coming up soon?'

'Oh, it hasn't got to that stage yet.'

'Good, because I wouldn't mind having a conversation with you. It seems it might have to wait until Monday morning anyway.'

She thought he had finished but as she was making her way out of his office, he said, 'Because, you know . . . I . . . we . . . would miss you like mad.'

Perhaps it was just the kind of sentiment, for form's sake, that employers always express. But somehow, to her ears, he had conveyed it with quite a bit of feeling. In hindsight it amused her though, picturing him standing there in his shorts looking for all the world like an overgrown boy scout.

Although naturally he tried to hide it from others, Frank had to confess to himself he was feeling as nervous as a kitten about the opening match the next day. It was probably better that it was at home and against opposition that had ended last season only three places above Oakhill. The trouble with this kind of thinking, though, was that it could give added pressure to win. For if they didn't win home games of this sort, what chance would they have against better teams?

The other main anxiety rattling around in Frank's head was that, although he had been at the club a few weeks already, he hadn't carried out anything like the normal pre-season preparations he would have done at other clubs he'd managed. All his energies seemed to have been taken up by things going on behind the scenes. It was only in the last fortnight or so that he had felt able to start sorting out what was happening on the field. Even during that short space of time, it had seemed like one long battle after another to try and win the hearts and minds of players. The fact that Bennison and Carpenter had so obviously boosted the strength of the team only served to make so-called senior pros, like full-back Jed Forrester and one or two of the midfield players, seemingly even more determined to stick to 'traditional' Oakhill United ways. This could not help but rub off on younger players like Trentham and Shanahan. With difficulties compounded by having to work alongside Steele, the team was still pulling in too many different directions for his liking.

He could really have done with making sure he stayed completely relaxed the evening before the match. But, impossible as it was to put out of mind, he had agreed to going out to dinner with Rosie. Much as he had enjoyed it the previous week, he had to admit to feeling rather more constrained this time round. For one thing, their meeting last Friday had had a spontaneity to it. There just hadn't been time to think. This week, particularly with all the hype in the papers about it being his first big game with the club, it occurred to him he would be running a much greater risk this week of drawing unnecessary attention to himself. Being seen out in the company of a dazzling-looking younger woman was one thing but another factor was that Rosie had an obvious connection with the club through her son Ben. It certainly wouldn't look very good for example if Matt, in his Academy role, were to learn he had been seen cavorting around with the boy's mother!

So when he received a text from Rosie, as he was just about to set off home from work, it seemed like she must have been reading his mind perfectly:

> *U must have thoughts on match tomorrow.*
> *If too busy, don't mind putting off our dinner date.*
> *Maybe u like just come round for*
> *glass of fizz? A toast to the new season?!*
> *Time to suit u . . .? Don't worry, u can relax,*
> *Ben out from 5 onwards.*

It felt like a weight lifted off his mind, and the revised arrangement sounded ideal. He immediately sent back a message saying it all sounded perfect and that he'd aim to be there for seven o'clock. Moments later he received a text saying:

> *See u at 7 x*

Again, while admitting it shouldn't have seemed such a big thing that she had chosen to attach the 'x' at the end, it still hadn't stopped him punching the air, much as if Oakhill had put the ball in the back of the opposition net. Somehow, the prospect of being in Rosie's company again had the power to lift him free of his worries.

After their brief exchange of texts, he now felt no hint of his earlier trepidation. And when it reached the time to saunter his way across the road, he felt much in the same mood as he had done the previous week.

'It's lovely to see you again!' She had greeted him at the door with as welcoming a smile as ever.

'Yes,' he replied, as usual tongue-tied in her presence but feeling an enormous sense of pleasure from the impact of seeing her again. His eyes quickly took in a tight-fitting sweater and elegantly cut trousers which as always served to accentuate her shapeliness. The truth was though, he suspected, she could have pulled a black bin liner over her head and he still would have found her unutterably attractive.

No sooner was he over the threshold than she was opening a bottle of bubbly.

'Isn't it lovely to be together again at the end of another week?' she said almost cooingly as she tossed her prettily curled hair back to help withstand the explosive sound of the cork popping.

'To Oakhill United and a successful season!'

'To Oakhill United!' he echoed the sentiment.

'Let's take our drink upstairs,' she said, leading the way up the first flight of stairs from the kitchen to the lounge. Following in her footsteps, he was absorbed by watching the back of her striking pair of high heels as she negotiated the stairs in front of him.

'So how do you think we're doing?' she asked when they reached the lounge.

'Perfectly, I think!' he answered with a candour that surprised him.

'Do you think we'll get promotion this year?'

138

Oh! She was meaning the football! He would have to watch more carefully which track his mind wandered onto. As for promotion, they'd be lucky to stay in existence.

'Well I wouldn't be sure of that,' he said.

'Ben is so much better you know. The way he is now, I've promised to take him away on holiday again soon. So long as his father puts up some of the money. I need to get in touch to see if he will. But I can't tell you how much Ben has improved,' she said, with a look of ecstatic happiness on her face, clearly warming to her theme.

'Mm?' He sensed a familiar, detailed account coming on of Ben's utter transformation. Frank merely kept on nodding his head in appreciation. Only, at a certain point, he had found himself unexpectedly interrupting and suddenly asking without any relevance whatsoever to what she was saying, 'Is there a man in your life?'

She looked back at him, momentarily surprised by the unexpected directness of his question.

'No, there isn't,' she replied in a tone as definite as if he had asked her, 'Is there an elephant in the room?'

He was half expecting she might have reciprocated by asking him a similar question back, but disappointingly, she didn't. Instead, to his slight consternation, she then carried on talking in much the same way as before. He supposed, though, it showed he couldn't have struck her as too gauche in what he had said. All he knew was that he had felt almost desperate to ask her the question. In the end he was pleased that he had done. For if anything, the atmosphere seemed to become even more relaxed between them as the evening went on.

Later on, as the time came for him to leave, she led him out of the lounge. Fleetingly, as they reached the staircase, he thought her eyes glanced up rather than down the stairs. In the event, her step unerringly took her back downwards towards the front door.

'Goodnight Frank. I know you've probably had your mind all

evening on the match tomorrow,' she said, as they were about to part, 'but can I just give you a small hug? To wish good luck for tomorrow!'

Stretching up on her high heels, the warmth of her body embraced him like the heat of intense sunrays burning through him.

Walking the short distance back to his house, it seemed like he was gasping for air. If he had any part of his mind on the match at all that moment, it definitely felt as though the team was 2-0 up already.

17

Frank would have felt better about his pre-match pep talk to the players if he hadn't been interrupted by the Chairman while in full flow. He would not have begrudged it if Arnold Preston had merely wanted to pop his head round the changing room door and wish the team well at the start of the season. But of course the Chair could never keep it simply to a brief cheery 'Good Luck!', leave it at that and be on his way. No, he had to stick around, going to great lengths to remind the players of the club's illustrious past deeds. Then totally oblivious to what might or might not have been happening before, the Chair had chosen to hand over to Simon Steele. Taken completely by surprise, Simon had gurgled before trotting out a few of his usual tried and trusted homilies, like 'set out like the clappers' and 'give it 110% effort'.

In practical terms, the whole atmosphere and effect of what Frank had been saying before Arnold Preston had chosen to appear on the scene ten minutes from kick-off had evaporated like air out of a punctured football. By the time he had chance to pick up the pieces of his delivery again, only Bennison and Carpenter still seemed to be at all on his wavelength.

Frank always prided himself on his powers to motivate players to go out on the field of play with a solid match-plan etched in their minds. As well, he liked to work them up, with the odd bit of taunting if necessary, to visualise themselves as winners and to talk it through with them step-by-step, what it would take for them to achieve the desired outcome. It was about building up an insatiable appetite for the game ahead. But on this occasion, as his team trooped out of the changing room onto the field of play, Frank had a kind of hollow foreboding deep inside him that, despite all their show of taking the game seriously, as a team they were still lacking the necessary hunger and focus.

Frank has purposely decided beforehand to take a seat in the stand, at least to start with. This is to allow Simon Steele sole occupancy of the technical area on the edge of the pitch. This obviously suits Simon because, above all else, he craves to be seen as the one nearest to the action on the field of play. Frank has agreed to play the more detached role of observer and to feed back his comments in the changing room at half-time. He knows this is sacrificing his chance to affect things while play is going on but he also appreciates it might be confusing for players to see both managers standing on the touchline. In any case, for the first match of the season at least, Frank does not want it to look as if he is deliberately taking over. He is still hoping it will be possible for his and Simon's approaches to complement one another . . .

No sooner has Frank taken his seat than the referee has blown his whistle. In the spirit of New Year's Eve at midnight, the crowd lets off a special cheer in recognition of the start of the brand new season.

If only, though, games could succeed in living up to prior hopes and expectations! Squirming in his seat, Frank can only look on in acute discomfort as the first five minutes unfold with what can only be described as scrappy play between these two undistinguished sides. Apart from the lack of any real pattern emerging on the field of play, the main thing Frank notices is that the smaller number of travelling fans from Saxby are making their presence felt in a far more vociferous way than the quiet ranks of home supporters.

Then, seemingly from nowhere, a long ball is pumped up towards the Oakhill penalty area. As far as Frank can see, the Saxby striker is blatantly backing into the defender before theatrically collapsing on the edge of the penalty area, but managing somehow to wave his arms around in the general direction of the referee. However clumsy the appeal, it is instantly picked up on by a clamorous, baying noise from the tight-knit army of away fans congregating at that end of the pitch. To every Oakhill supporter's utter astonishment and disbelief, the referee runs up and signals a direct free kick to Saxby just outside the box, at the same time extending a yellow card to Price.

For the next three minutes, a messy pantomime ensues in which the referee persists in telling the Oakhill defensive wall it is not standing the regulation ten metres back. Meanwhile, a Saxby player is intent on lining his shot up on goal. At this point, Jed Forrester seems hell-bent on making his mark on the game. Taking it upon himself to orchestrate the defensive operation, Jed is now locked in argument with his keeper as to whether the wall is in the right position or not. Facing in the wrong direction, he has failed to respond to the referee's repeated instructions to all Oakhill defenders to retreat the full ten metres. Jed Forrester picks up a yellow card as if it is the most natural thing in the world for him to do. Frank reflects woefully that Jed must be intent on beating his existing League 2 record from last season!

When, finally, the referee blows his whistle for the free kick to be taken, the Saxby player coolly arches the ball over the wall and past the helpless outstretched arms of Harris into the top right-hand corner of the goal. Frank snatches a glance at his watch. Eight minutes gone, three of which the ball has technically been out of play, and Oakhill are 1-0 down at home to a team of fellow no-hopers!

While the away fans celebrate handsomely, Frank picks up routine displeasure from home fans aimed at the referee, with gallows humour such as 'Should've gone to Specsavers!' But also he can't help but pick up more acidic remarks like 'What a flaming shower!' and 'Same bloody story as last year!' and worse, much worse.

From whatever instinct, Frank's eye nervously drifts over to the relatively cocooned Director's Box where Arnold Preston is sitting in state in his Chairman's seat. As he uses his folded match programme to swat his knee to demonstrate a measured degree of frustration, Frank gains the impression that, to Arnold, the goal constitutes only a very minor setback in the overall context of the 125-year history of Oakhill United. The remaining directors, who Frank can recall from the Board meeting, are sitting either side of Arnold or in the row behind. Frank fails, though, to see Shazad Ali among their company. Still keeping his powder dry, no doubt.

For the next five minutes, with the home crowd feeling perhaps a bit guilty and at last trying to summon up the energy to get behind their team a bit, Oakhill start to carry the game to Saxby. But despite making certain inroads, Bennison and Carpenter are clearly finding it tough going being outnumbered by opposition defenders. All that Oakhill manage for their efforts is a couple of corners. But both are headed out with consummate ease by Saxby defenders.

Then the away team go relentlessly on the offensive and Oakhill's midfield is being sliced through like butter. This in turn puts the back four under the most intense of pressure. As chances pile up, it is only a matter of time before Saxby add to their lead. When the referee finally blows his whistle for half-time, the score has stretched to 3-0 and it seems to Frank almost as if Oakhill United have been let off lightly.

Raising himself from his seat, it isn't just the odd catcall he can hear around him. Instead, the Oakhill team leaves the field to boos and other contemptuous noises from every corner of the ground.

Despite all his experience, Frank feels very unsure what he can possibly say in the changing room to make one scrap of difference. Only he has been in the game long enough to know he has to give it his best shot.

'Not good is it? What do you think?' Simon Steele puts to Frank.

'No pressure then!'

Simon allows a flicker of a smile to show on his face. He understands the attempt on Frank's part not to appear totally at a loss to know what to do next.

'Think there's only one thing for it,' Frank says decisively.

Simon looks relieved to hear a plan exists at all. But then he is interested to know what it might be.

'We sub Forrester, Wilson, and Bolland, and give the young lads on the bench a full second half.'

Simon's jaw drops six inches.

'Take three off? And those three? The senior pros?'

'Even at this level, they're has-beens.'

'Are you going to say it, then?'

'I don't mind. You can if you want to,' Frank offers.

'No, I'll leave it to you.'

'But we are in agreement?'

'At three-nil down, we're running out of options, aren't we?'

'The only other thing is that we need to bring Bennison back into a holding midfield role rather than having him up front with Carpenter,' Frank puts forward.

'OK, but don't we need to score goals?'

'If Bennison steadies midfield, the lads coming on at half-time can go forward. We'll just have to see. By the way, I'll join you in the dugout for the second half.'

One last thing occurs to Frank to mention as the two of them finish their snatched conversation on their way to the changing room.

'I realise this is a high-risk strategy because if anyone gets injured second half, we've used all our substitutes. But . . .'

Mouth still agape, Simon waits to hear Frank's thinking.

'I firmly believe a point has to be made to the time-servers in our team that they're utterly dispensable.'

'Rather you than me!' Simon mutters as Frank sticks his chest out and pushes through the changing room door to get at the players.

145

For a few seconds, Frank doesn't say anything. He wants to settle them first. Then he will tear a strip off them.

'That was bloody awful!'

He looks round the room to make sure the point is sinking in. Then suddenly Forrester says, 'The ref should never have given that bloody free kick!'

'You reckon?' Frank comes back at him. 'Well he did! Anyway we haven't got time to go into that now. It's what we do in the second half that's going to count.'

The players all look apprehensive, much as Simon had when Frank had said there was only one thing for it.

'Forrester, Wilson and Bolland are coming off for the second half. Instead Mellor, Ramsden and Craig are coming off the bench and going on in their places.'

'But that's fucking barmy!' Jed Forrester instantly protests. 'For one thing, what happens if there's an injury?'

Frank and Simon share a quick knowing glance.

'That's a chance management is taking. The other change is that you, Tony, will play in a defensive midfield role just in front of the back four. That will release the four in midfield, Ramsden, Riley, Craig and Shanahan to attack. Three-nil down, we've got to go for it! Any questions? If not, let's give it our all this second half. We can do it you know. We can get back in this game if we all give it our best shot!'

He thinks he had better shut up at that point. There's a risk of overcomplicating things. Just as he is going back out through the door he hears the crash of an object thrown against the wall.

'Fucking disgrace if you ask me!' Jed Forrester is shouting out, sitting there with only one boot on. The other is on the floor by the side of the wall.

'No-one's asking you,' Frank replies coolly.

Right from the start of the second half, it is obvious that Oakhill are far more in control. Bennison is constantly breaking up Saxby attacks and laying the ball off cleverly to others. The players who have come on as substitutes are succeeding in finding space and looking hungry for the ball. Oakhill go close once or twice before Shanahan spins away from his opposite number and goes on a long, mazy run down the left wing. Reaching the bye-line, he crosses the ball to the far post and there is Carpenter meeting it firmly with his forehead and, from five metres out, giving the keeper no chance. Suddenly there is new hope. Frank and Simon rush to the touchline and exchange high fives with players by way of celebration. For the first time in the game, Saxby's heads drop and their rabid following goes quiet.

Meanwhile, the change in the home crowd is astonishing. For most of the first half there was a funereal silence. It is notice-able with Carpenter's goal that the crowd has picked up and is now giving the team their full backing. Saxby, for their part have started the second half complacently. Nursing a 3-0 lead, it looks to Frank as if they think they have already done enough. From the touchline, he inspires and urges the players on. It had felt terrible sitting up in the stand watching from a distance in the first half. Now he is beginning to feel he is doing a proper manager's job. The players on the pitch seem to be responding positively to all his comments and encouragement.

The opposition manager realises there is a game on and he too starts trying to whip his players up to make a greater effort. But the initiative is now firmly with Oakhill. Carpenter is looking particularly dangerous as if he means to add to his tally as fast as he can.

Signs of frustration are creeping into Saxby's game. Tackles are missed and 50-50 balls are going Oakhill's way. To the ironic cheers of the home crowd, the referee books a Saxby midfielder for a late challenge which leaves Ramsden sprawled out on the turf. From the resulting free kick, a massive appeal for hand-ball goes up and the referee points to the spot. Players look to the bench to see who will be entrusted. Frank shouts over to Tony to take it. After a short delay, during which the opposi-tion keeper is yellow-carded for gamesmanship, Tony sends him the wrong way, slotting the ball into the corner of the net to make it 3-2.

Frank glances at his watch and sees there are still twenty minutes left. Bennison gains possession from Saxby's kick-off and is prompting yet another attack on the opposition goal. The ball goes out to Ramsden on the right who controls it, looks up and tries to pick out a late run from Riley on the near post. Unfortunately, just as the cross arrives, there is a sickening clash of heads as Riley and a Saxby defender collide. Both players lie prone on the ground while medical assistants rush to their aid. It is clear that both players are seriously injured with head wounds and likely concussion. Eventually, both are stretchered off.

'Told you this would happen!' Frank hears Jed Forrester turn round to say to the other two players who were subbed at half-time. Frank knows it's meant for his ears.

Meanwhile, Saxby bring on a substitute and Oakhill are at an obvious disadvantage with only ten men on the field. Even so, they keep on playing with great enthusiasm and, three minutes before the end, Carpenter hits a post. But, despite everyone's efforts, the ball will not go in the net. Six minutes of injury time are played, during which Oakhill throw everything at the Saxby goal. But eventually, the referee standing in the middle of the pitch blows his whistle to bring the match to an end.

Frank knew he was bound to take some stick for the decision to bring all three subs on at half-time. But, even as he had time to reflect on things in the evening, he felt quite unrepentant at what he had done. If he regretted anything at all, it was that he picked Forrester, Wilson and Bolland in the first place! To be fair to himself though, he probably needed to give it one game to see what the team he had inherited was up to. Even if, in the event, it had ended up being only half a game. But at least he knew he could never go back to picking the same team as had started out against Saxby. His resolve was to erase the memory of the first half from his mind completely and instead to build on the successes of the second half that had been there for all to see. That was how he hoped others would see it too . . . but then experience had already taught him that at Oakhill United you could never take anything for granted.

An opening home 3-2 defeat was certainly not the most auspicious of starts but Frank was not down. Later on in the evening, after three or four glasses of red wine, with his feet up watching Match of the Day he somehow felt able to see things in healthier perspective.

18

To say they'd lost the first game of the season at home to fellow-strugglers Saxby, Frank reckoned he'd got off fairly lightly in *The Oakhill Times* report on the Monday. Thankfully, the reporter had taken much greater store by the second-half recovery than the first-half debacle. As far as Frank's controversial half-time substitutions were concerned, he had used the post-match interview with the reporter to good effect to justify the thinking behind his decision. The paper liked to run what they called a 'Fan Poll' and it had been reassuring to see that the question 'Was it right to make the half-time substitutions?' had a 76% 'Yes' compared with a 24% 'No' approval rating.

But that was yesterday's copy. Meanwhile today, Tuesday, the paper had its biggest scoop in decades with the banner headline screaming across the top of the front page: *OAKHILL UNITED: DEBT IN MILLIONS!*

Frank learned from Simon that the Chair was incandescent with rage, not with the headline but the fact a Board member must have leaked the Auditors' Report to the local press. After all, only Board members had received a copy so far.

Frank naturally had a shrewd suspicion what must have happened, even though he was wholly intent on keeping his thinking to himself. He felt glad though that he couldn't personally be held accountable, not least because he hadn't yet been given a copy of the Report. When the reporter had rung him earlier that morning, he had been able to reply in perfect innocence that he knew nothing of the Report findings.

Arnold Preston had seen fit to bring forward the Board meeting from Tuesday next week to Thursday this week. Frank realised he would have to be in touch with Shazad sometime before then.

Meanwhile, the club's plight was laid bare in the coverage of the storyline that extended four pages deep into that afternoon's edition. Apart from the fact it was in debt to the tune of over two million pounds, reference was made to the fact that Jack Hubbard had been suspended pending further investigation into 'financial irregularities'. The possible docking of points was also mentioned which, given the fact that Oakhill had none whatso-ever at the moment, couldn't help but elicit a wry smile on Frank's face. If the club should be compelled to forfeit as many as twelve points, say, it could take virtually the whole of the remaining season just to claw back from a negative to a positive figure.

But the worst scenario portrayed was that of the club plum-meting out of existence. The paper of course concentrated its more sensationalist coverage on this angle: that this disastrous Report would write the final chapter in the club's long, proud, 125-year history. It was spelt out in no uncertain terms that the only way the club could survive in its present form was if a cred-ible buyer could be found within a matter of days. Significantly, Frank noticed that the paper made no effort to speculate about possible buyers. That presumably was a subject which could be saved up for further editions later on in the week.

Otherwise, apart from specific details of the Auditors' Report itself, most of today's edition looked to pick up on the reaction of the Chairman of the club himself. In predictable fashion, Arnold Preston declined to make any comment until the Report itself had been officially released. The only element he had been willing to concede was that the Business Manager was suspended.

Bearing in mind the effect the story was bound to have on players, Simon had informed Frank that Arnold Preston was calling a meeting with them the next morning. It didn't bear thinking what mood they would be in for the midweek game later on in the evening. Luckily, it was at a ground no more than fifteen miles away. But straight after the meeting with the Chair they would be climbing onto the bus. Frank only hoped the players were capable of shutting the situation out of their minds for the ninety minutes of the game.

In the process of opening Frank's correspondence, Emily had come across a letter addressed to him containing a request for a reference on her own behalf from the council. She wasn't sure whether to mention it when she took his mail through to him. If she did, it might look like she was seeking to put some kind of pressure on. If she didn't, the mail might just pass him by completely and end up festering in his in-tray for days on end.

It was probably because he had been so intensely busy of late that his in-tray was suffering neglect. She had naturally offered to do as much of his work for him as possible on the administrative side. But she hardly supposed she could write her own reference.

In the end, she had decided to try and be subtle and just make passing mention of the chat he had said he wanted with her yesterday, but which hadn't yet materialised. She was actually quite curious to know what it might be about. But he must now have his mind firmly on the mid-week game. Perhaps he had just forgotten or suddenly it didn't seem so important in the general scheme of things.

To add to everything else, there was the bombshell of the Auditors' Report. As required by the Chair, she had slipped copies into envelopes to post off to Board members late on Friday. Printing the name of Jed Forrester on one of these, she naturally surmised the contents of the reports would spread like wildfire round the club upon his breaking the seal.

Normally she supposed it would have been Jack Hubbard, in his role as Business Manager, who would have detailed her what to do, rather than the Chair himself. In fact, Jack's absence had continued to puzzle her, particularly when his desk looked as if it had been cleared. Despite seeking to keep herself at arm's length as far as possible, she couldn't help but detect massive tensions beneath the surface throughout the club.

Frank almost pounced on her when she stepped into his office.

'We really must have that conversation I said we needed to have,' he said, leaping to his feet like an evangelist preacher. It felt like she were under some kind of attack.

'Look, you can't go for that job.'

Her puzzled expression failed to have any disarming effect, as he blazed on, 'Because you're needed here!'

Oh, it was as simple as that, was it? she thought to herself.

'But for how long?' she questioned. 'The other job I'm going for is permanent.'

'Well, this one here could be.'

'Which one here exactly?' However strangely put, it seemed the only way to make her point. In addition, she felt tempted to mention he hadn't referred once yet to Jack Hubbard's situation.

'The job of Business Manager of course.'

Nor did she care to slip in at this point that it seemed the whole club was currently under threat from a winding-up order.

'If, that is . . .' he let out enthusiastically, but seemed to lose his drift completely. Then he resumed, but much more hesitantly, 'At the very least, you could be Acting Business Manager for as long as you're due to remain with us till you go on your holiday in Italy.'

In one way she couldn't deny feeling impressed that he was showing so much interest in her. However, bending over backwards to be fair to herself, she knew very well that if she were successful in gaining the post at the council, the amount of notice she would need to serve at Oakhill United Football Club was minimal.

Undeniably, it was very flattering to hear Frank talking like this. Job-wise though, she knew which side her bread was buttered. In short, if she were successful in her application to the council, she would be foolish not to take up their offer.

'So you're not at all interested in what we have to offer here?'

How dare he present her with a conclusion like that? For a moment she felt at a loss to know how to respond.

'I'll give it serious thought,' she said, fully realising she wasn't responding as compliantly as he might have hoped.

At the end of this exchange, she felt she had more than held her own. She also couldn't deny feeling a certain thrill. However strongly his insecurity had conveyed itself, it was still up to her to survey the whole situation seriously before committing herself one way or the other.

On the one hand, she could press on with her application for the council post. On the other, it was obvious to her from what Frank had said he seemed keen to keep her at Oakhill. Whatever happened though, it mattered a lot to her that he seemed to be taking proper notice of her at last.

'All systems go. Everything is in place!'

He noted straight away Shazad was back to his usual brash self. Frank had travelled over to Manchester in the hope of meeting one or two others in the consortium. 'The consortium' which was always being referred to. But it was Shazad on his own again.

'You know the Board meeting has been brought forward to two days' time on Thursday, don't you?' He was keen to bring it to Frank's attention.

'Yes, so I gather.'

'I'll definitely be there myself.'

Well after the last fiasco, that was a relief to hear.

'We've been in touch with the auditors already. They will be the ones charged with looking into the viability of any new buyers coming forward.'

Shazad strove to hold Frank's attention as if with new-found confidence. For Frank's own part, he wasn't feeling too disposed to hearing more businessman's bluster. He had made the trip across this evening to hear some actual detail.

'Do you mind if I ask you some questions?' Frank cut in, knowing he risked sounding rude and impatient.

'Why yes Frank, of course.'

154

'I thought I might be meeting one or two of the others in your consortium at some point. Er, like this evening?'

Shazad scratched his chin uneasily.

'I'll be honest with you. Although I keep telling them to say now you're the man for the job, they want to do thing in stages. The first thing is achieving the take-over. Then it's getting down to the detail. We're hoping to take the club over before the weekend.'

'Can I ask you where all this leaves the players I've brought to Oakhill United?'

'We want to keep them. But we want to get rid of rubbish and bring in more players.'

That was telling it straight.

'How about Simon Steele?'

'Of course I have to ask your opinion. How you find him?' Shazad fired back at him. Frank did not know whether this was a courtesy question.

'Well, actually, I think he's come on quite a bit.' How odd it seemed to hear himself making out a defence for the young man who he had found so arrogant on first impression. Perhaps he was feeling sorry for him, with his large mortgage to pay back.

'But not enough, we don't think!' Shazad cut in ruthlessly. 'The management team we'd want is yourself with Bennison as player-manager.'

Now the other man was talking! Together, he and Bennison would make a good team. A rapport was already established between them.

'I do feel a bit sorry for Simon Steele, though. He's been a bit in the pocket of the Chair,' Frank said, inclined for some strange reason to go the extra mile in pointing out the difficulties he had inevitably faced during his short period as a manager.

'We're not employing a manager who feels sorry for anyone. We want winners. If I were you, Frank, I'd have a word with Bennison before Thursday and see whether he's up for it.'

*   *   *

The last thing Frank had wanted to do was rush Tony Bennison into making a decision. But with the away match the following evening and the Board meeting on Thursday, there seemed little alternative but to speak to him tonight. At least then Tony could sleep on what was being put to him and get back to Frank the next morning.

When Frank had come out of his meeting with Shazad at 5.30 he had phoned Tony immediately. Admitting it was short notice, he had asked whether they could possibly meet up to discuss 'a certain matter'.

'Yes any time you like,' Tony said in his usual willing way.

'How about tonight in two hours' time?'

'Yes . . . of course.'

That was what he really appreciated about Tony. He was no-one's fool but he would follow Frank to the ends of the earth. However preposterous anything he said sounded, Tony always seemed to trust his judgement.

'Where?'

Oh god, he hadn't thought it through, had he? The only thing that came into his mind, not knowing the area very well, was to propose going to the same restaurant that Rosie had taken him to that Friday night.

'Do you know where it is?' he asked.

'Don't worry, boss, I'll see you there. What time?'

'7.30. I'll get back to you if there's any difficulty booking a table but otherwise, see you there.'

'7.30 it is!'

Bearing in mind it was a Tuesday, booking the table had been no problem. At 7.35, Tony was already there and they took a leisurely drink at the bar.

Five or ten minutes later, they moved through into the restaurant. Greeted by the head waiter, they were being escorted to their table when Frank's attention unexpectedly became distracted. It wasn't as if there were many people sitting there in the restaurant. But having said that, his mind wasn't in the least prepared for Rosie Skipton to be one of them! She was seated at table with a man, in whose company she appeared to be positively revelling.

Although the man had his back to him, the only thing Frank couldn't help picking out was that he looked about the same age as Rosie. Definitely much younger than himself.

Luckily Rosie didn't seem to catch sight of him. Perhaps it was because she was so wrapped up in talking to the man. In the way Frank had come to adore so much, the expression on her face was vibrant and compelling.

In a moment of blind panic, he had turned back from the restaurant entrance and retreated to a spot in the bar where he was safely out of view. The simple truth was that he hadn't been able to stomach the sight of Rosie with someone else. The only way was to avoid the situation altogether.

Meanwhile, Tony followed him back out of the restaurant looking mystified. Accustomed over the years to the quirkiness of some of his tactical moves on the football field, on this occasion he could only stare at Frank, bemused.

'Do you know, all of a sudden, I don't feel hungry,' was the best Frank could come up with.

'All right. Shall we just have a drink then?' Tony had replied accommodatingly, his eyes switching uneasily between bar and restaurant, wondering how a man's appetite could have entirely disappeared within such a short distance.

'That would be fine,' Frank said, just beginning to pull himself together again, 'but I think it'd be better somewhere else if you don't mind.'

Tony had a responsive sense of humour and couldn't help laughing out loud. 'It was you who chose the place! Don't tell me, when we get to "somewhere else", you're going to say you're not feeling thirsty?' Meanwhile he went on staring round the place as if he were missing something like a bomb waiting to go off. 'Looks a decent enough place to me,' he concluded, scratching his head.

'Yes, well, if we're not eating, I thought I'd rather go to a pub.'

Frank knew he was beginning to sound plainly ridiculous now. But, however closely he had worked with the other man over a period of time, his pride or whatever, made it impossible to tell Tony the real reason why he was behaving like a teenage schoolboy.

'Got anywhere in mind then?' Tony felt inclined to ask, knowing for a fact that neither of them could exactly claim to know their way round Oakhill.

'There's bound to be a decent pub around this part of town. Let's go.'

Desperately trying to put his eccentric-seeming behaviour behind him, Frank naturally felt a fair bit relieved after managing to escape the restaurant. The pair of them had to walk up and down several streets though before coming across a decent-looking pub. In all this time, Frank realised how much he was trying Tony's patience. It was patently unfair keeping him in this state of suspense.

So as soon as they had found somewhere and he had bought a half-pint of lager each, he waded straight in. 'How do you fancy being promoted to player-manager?'

Tony glanced back at him as if fazed out of his mind. 'I think I know why you've been acting so strangely tonight! You're having me on, aren't you? You've finally flipped, haven't you?'

'Look I'm serious, Tony. That's what the new owners say they're looking at. Me Executive Manager and you player-manager.'

'Where does that leave Simon Steele?'

'Where do you think?'

Tony scratched his chin again. Things seemed to be getting ever more puzzling as the evening wore on.

'Why yes of course I'd be interested!'

'That's all I need to know for the time being.'

For the rest of the conversation they had that evening, Frank couldn't help but feel a sense of gratification as to how excited Tony felt about the prospect of stepping up to management. It was always good to feel you were advancing the cause of people like Tony who were so worthy of the chance.

It was 10 o'clock when Frank finally made his way back home. But for all the importance of the conversation he had had with Tony, there was still one more important thing on his mind.

19

Although it continued to prey on him that he had seen Rosie out with another man, Frank had done his level best to shut it out of his mind in the meantime. At the time, not least being in a pub, his first instinct had been to cut loose and have a few drinks. But he had stayed disciplined. He and Tony had kept it down to a half of lager each before they'd gone on to soft drinks. Frank knew it wasn't necessary for himself as manager to keep so strictly off the booze. After all, he wasn't the one having to perform the next day on the field of play. But he recognised how hard it would have been for Tony having to restrict himself while the other man indulged. With tomorrow being a match day, the least Frank could do was set a good example.

He had steeled himself to drive directly back to his house and completely rule out the barest curiosity he might have in relation to 3 Queen's Anne Way. This he had managed to do only with the most massive of constraint. Negotiating the short passage between the car and his front door, he had to close his eyes to prevent himself indulging in an almost irresistible instinct to glance down the road.

But having successfully achieved the aim of getting safely back within the four walls of his house, he found himself gradually becoming more and more agitated. At first, he had sat quietly in his armchair reading a sports magazine to try and maintain an inner calmness. But whenever he heard the sound of a car passing the house, it inevitably connected itself up in his mind with Rosie. So then he had switched on the television to help drown out any distracting noise from outside. However, just as the news bulletin was coming to an end, he heard the roar of a sports-car engine and the screeching of brakes a short distance down the road.

Like a flash he jumped out of his chair and ran down the stairs. Opening the front door as quietly as he could, he switched off the outside light and stood there transfixed as Rosie emerged from the driver's side of the car and a man eased himself out of the nearby passenger side. As he saw her fumbling in her handbag for the house key, he heard the man say something which made her laugh. It wasn't difficult to tell they were continuing to have a good time. With a hollow feeling inside, he then saw and heard the door close quietly behind them. But to Frank, in self-torment, it felt as if it had been slammed in his face.

He continued to stand there in the dark as the lights switched on inside No. 3 in quick succession from the ground floor up to the first floor. And then fifteen minutes later, causing him a painful, sinking feeling because he was absolutely dreading it, the second floor suddenly sprang to light. For a horrific, fleeting moment, he glimpsed Rosie closing curtains and he even caught sight of the man behind her. To spare himself further torture, he went back inside.

Desperately feeling the need for a resuscitating glass of wine, his immediate apprehension was that there was none in the house. Gratefully though, he recalled he had stocked up at the super-market over the weekend. Seeing numerous bottles on the rack, he felt all too well aware that if he were to start drinking at this late hour, he had better set himself a quota for his own good. Sizing up his mental state, he decided strictly to keep it to two glasses. However, the unfortunate thing was that when it came to the second glass, it had tasted so good that he was very soon pouring his third.

It was about midnight, after five glasses, that the combined emotions of angst and self-pity had eventually kicked in. He resisted a terrible impulse to go and stand out on the street adjacent to

3 Queen Anne's Way and lob stones up at the second floor window. Instead he had picked up his mobile from the table at his side, toying with the idea of sending her a text.

The effect of the wine had almost thoroughly paralysed his inhibitions and he was feeling in a frame of mind to let her have the low-down as to how bitterly disappointed he was at what, albeit unbeknown to her, he had witnessed tonight.

Adding to his complete sense of powerlessness was the assumption that she probably wouldn't get to read his text until the next morning. But he still couldn't rid his head of the urge to have some kind of message stored up for her. In his present state of mind, irrespective of the fact it was now into the early hours of the morning, he wanted nothing more than to fire a shot across her bows to register his indignation. But what exactly should he say? Perhaps, by now, his mind wasn't at its sharpest? In the end, having dismissed one or two more dramatically worded forms of accusation, he typed in:

Trusted you when you said there wasn't any other man in your life!

Pausing a few seconds to decide whether to commit himself, he finally closed his eyes and pressed the 'send' button.

There, he had done it! Nor could he help feeling a strangely satisfying sense of relief at having committed himself by way of a reaction. In his mind's eye, she would probably wonder a little what he was getting at, but then she was bound to realise he felt hurt in some way. That was the main thing he was seeking to convey. At that point in the evening, with sleep finally beckoning, he sensed it would have killed him to have had to suffocate all the wretched instincts welling up inside him. Slipping the mobile back onto the table, he was on his way to the stairs when he was startled by the sound of it throbbing back to life. Oh my god, it couldn't be a call back so soon, could it?

He looked at his watch and it said 1:56. It couldn't be anyone else calling him at that hour. Suddenly, it crashed in on him how utterly senseless it had been for him to send any message at all.

On tiptoe, he crept back to the table watching the mobile all the while as if it were a landmine waiting to go off at the slightest of touches. Picking it up gently, he saw from the number on the face that the message was indeed from Rosie. Some new instinct told him that, however anguished he had felt prior to sending his own message, it would be nothing compared to how he would feel after pressing the button to receive her message back. The thought even occurred to him that it might be better to let it wait now till the morning to see what she had said in response. But by this point he was far too desperately keen to know the score. Dead set on detonating the mine, he pressed the button and surveyed the fallout:

> *How dare you talk to me like that? I am not your wife. Do not*
> *text me again under any circumstances.*

That was it, then? He had blown it. Crawling up the stairs to his bed, he just wanted to sink his head into the pillow and seek oblivion.

Arnold Preston knew that he and the football club he loved were both in a bit of a hole. But he had built his reputation on being a fighter, not a quitter. Yes, it was the most serious challenge he had faced in the seven years he had been chairman of the club. He wasn't going to run away from the situation though. Made of sterner stuff, he belonged to the community of Oakhill through and through. He would do everything possible to avert the crisis and get the club back on an even keel again.

But drastic situations called for drastic remedies. First of all, there was the nonsense in his mind of the club having taken on Frank Borrow. The club hadn't been able to afford much of a salary to put up for Simon Steele when he had been appointed to the job of manager under proper procedures. Now, the stupidity of having taken on Frank Borrow as a so-called Executive Manager was plain for everyone to see. Even if Borrow had made one or two improvements in some people's eyes, he for one hadn't been impressed. In particular, he didn't like his autocratic style of doing things behind the Board's back. Whenever he was asked his opinion of Frank Borrow, Arnold would look meaningfully at the person before coming out with his favourite line, 'The only trophy he's going to pick up this year is the Brian Clough Award for Arrogance!'

It was typical of the young businessman Shazad to have thought it a good idea to recruit an Executive Manager. That was only because it sounded impressive. But all that had happened in Arnold's eyes, and equally so in the opinion of the players he respected who had been at the club for years, was that it confused everyone having two managers. The general feeling was that the team had known where they stood much better when there was only one boss. Looking back on things, Arnold knew how difficult it must have been for Simon having to have someone peering over his shoulder all the time. When he had spoken yesterday to him about how he was planning on getting rid of Frank Borrow, the young man naturally seemed delighted.

Even the players themselves had put in a complaint against Borrow. Arnold had convened a meeting tonight, the day before the Board meeting, to discuss the initial findings of the investigation being conducted by the three-man panel which of course he was chairing himself.

As for the signing-on of new players without going through proper procedures, the chickens were coming home to roost in that direction. Never mind any minor financial irregularities, it was obvious now that the club couldn't afford to take on Bennison and Carpenter. And how disrespectful had it been anyway for him to sub three established players at half-time in the first game of the season? Such a crazy move had in his view cost them the game through having to play much of the second half with only ten men. None of this gave any hope of stability at the club while the present Executive Manager remained in post.

Besides getting rid of Borrow, Arnold Preston had talked to a lot of local interests who he hoped might be willing to join together in coming up with a rescue package. The only trouble was that it might take a bit longer to put together. But he was still hoping to persuade the auditing people that it was a better long-term project having a home-grown group running the club rather than some cowboy outfit from outside. Hopefully, the audit representative would say something supportive of this nature at tomorrow's meeting.

Arnold hadn't been at all looking forward to having to address the players that morning, but he had to say he felt the meeting had gone as well as he could possibly have expected. Firstly, players like Jed Forrester had said they appreciated the fact he valued them enough to hold the meeting to explain the situation properly. However tense the occasion might have been, he hadn't detected any rancour directed against him personally. He was appreciative of that because it showed he still had their respect.

Wishing them well for tonight's away game, he assured them he would go on doing all he could to keep Oakhill Football Club 'alive and kicking'. When he used this phrase, a wry smile had appeared on the faces of one or two players but they knew where he was coming from. In short, they could trust him to keep things going the same way they had been for so many years previously. So long as he had anything to do with it, Oakhill would go on holding its head up high.

'Poker your game, boss?'

Frank felt the need to pinch himself! Could Jed Forrester be actually asking him to join the seasoned pros card school at the back of the bus? Honours didn't get any higher than this.

'You know what they say?' he replied.

'No?' Jed looked awkwardly at his best mate Mick Bolland.

'A fool and his money are easily parted. That's what happens when I play cards!'

'Season ticket for the boss, then. We love losers at our table, don't we, Mick?'

A huge laugh went up and down the bus. But then Frank or Jed could have said anything between them that evening and it would have struck a resounding chord. After all, it didn't get any better than travelling home having thrashed the opposition on their own ground 6-1!

The rub of it was that team selection had been the reverse of the game against Saxby. Tonight Frank had put out, at the start of the game, the same line-up that had played the second half the previous Saturday and clawed back the two goals. Luckily, Riley had recovered quickly from his injury at the weekend and was able to play.

Tonight, they'd picked up exactly where they'd left off in the last game. The first half had gone an absolute treat: 4-0 up at half-time. And this was against opposition who were second favourites, according to the bookies, to win the League 2 championship. Carpenter had been lethal and completed a hat-trick within the first twenty minutes. Then the young lad Trentham, playing at left-back, who was Frank's strongest advocate of the club's new training regime, had broken upfield to score the fourth after a fifty-metre run.

As the players sat there in the changing room at half-time feeling a tad jubilant, Frank had announced that three of the players would be replaced by Forrester, Wilson and Bolland, the exact same players of course who had been subbed in the first game. The look on Tony Bennison's face was one which Frank regretted not having on camera. In other words, what did mad Frank think he was doing this time?

Well, of course, it was taking a monumental risk. He probably wouldn't do it again after tonight. But he was making a statement, wasn't he? The fact was it gave a chance to those three players, who had felt discarded during the course of the first game, to prove themselves.

And prove themselves they did! Although the other team woke

up sufficiently to score a goal themselves halfway through the second half, Oakhill stretched their lead even further with late goals, both of which were scored by two of the substitutes, Forrester himself with a 35-yard screamer and his midfield henchman Bolland with more of a tap-in after an eight-man passing movement. Team Oakhill was even showing it had a range of methods of scoring goals at its disposal!

No wonder then that Frank, with such obvious man-management skills was now being urged to join Oakhill United's most prestigious card school. Definitely, he was beginning to feel accepted.

Meanwhile, amid all this euphoria the only one who looked a shade less than delighted was Simon Steele. Frank couldn't quite work it out. After all, thinking back to earlier in the day, Simon had seemed blissfully happy in the presence of the Chairman, Arnold Preston, when he had come to talk to the players.

Frank had to hand it to Arnold Preston, though. He definitely knew how to pitch things to calm everything down. Crisis, what crisis? He had a way with words that only politicians have. He could make the Black Death sound like a mere common cold. He had succeeded in conveying a message to the players that had the complete valium effect.

As always when the Chair was going off on one, Frank had felt inclined to keep his counsel. But he certainly wasn't prepared to give the players the same message when he had them to himself before the kick-off in the evening. He had let them have it both barrels. He had told them that if half the reports were true about how seriously the club was in debt, then they should take it they could be on the open market within forty-eight hours. How they played tonight was going to determine how any possible interested club might entertain the prospect of taking them on. In other words, play out of your skin or else!

Frank had to admit he was never into touchy-feely sentimentality. He had set out the challenge as honestly as he saw the situation himself. And look what had happened. They had played above themselves to the tune of a miraculous 6-1 win against highly-rated opposition!

Frank had done two things after the game which he now accepted were both reckless in the extreme. He had ventured to the back of the bus to join Jed Forrester's card school and duly lost £150 into the bargain. And then, on returning home, he had disregarded Rosie Skipton's stricture not to text her again 'under any circumstances' but sent the following message:

Please forgive me for last night!

Somehow, he knew losing the £150 would prove much less painful.

20

He had hoped and prayed for a message back from Rosie but in vain. He had even thought of sending her another text describing how well the match had gone. But each time he felt tempted, he fought back the instinct. One unreturned message was more than enough.

Unable to sleep, he lay in bed with his thoughts veering wildly from triumphant recollections of the 6-1 win to disastrous recriminations over how he had botched things up with Rosie. Although he could see now it served him right for reacting so stupidly, he still hoped he could correct things. At all costs, he shouldn't let irresponsible feelings of jealousy get the better of him. Having said that, he could not deny he was still very interested to know who the stranger was. As a punishment to himself for having this last thought, he switched his mobile off altogether.

Walking out to his car before setting off to work, he could not resist the temptation of looking down the road. The familiar red sports car wasn't there, so he assumed she had set off to work already. Even though he averted his eyes quickly, the bitter feeling of two nights ago wouldn't quite go away. Then, suspecting he had seen something unusual, he found himself looking back again. Was he hallucinating? Yes, his eyes might be deceiving him but what he thought he saw was a 'For Sale' board. Wanting to make sure he wasn't making a mistake, he walked down the road to check it wasn't perhaps outside No. 1 or perhaps No. 5. But no it was definitely outside No. 3!

It was such a shock to his system that he even started looking at the house for any sign of activity. Or had she done a midnight flit with her lover boy? What had he told himself about keeping jealousy in check?

When he got into work, he was going to make a point of seeing Matt Johnson to see if Ben Skipton might have said anything to him about a possible house move. But Emily told him *The Oakhill Times* reporter was waiting for him, so he decided to get that over with first.

'Fantastic result by the way!' Emily said, her eyes lighting up with pleasure. It felt very heartwarming to him that she seemed so personally pleased on his account.

'Well you can't complain about lack of copy from Oakhill United at the moment, can you?' he put to the waiting reporter.

'Yes, we're positively spoilt for choice, aren't we?' he chirped back as cockily as Frank could remember from the last time.

Frank was all too aware the story about the club's finances had gone on through from Monday, when it had first broken, to Wednesday's edition. No doubt, with the Board meeting tonight, it had the legs to run on much, much longer.

'You'll be glad to know we've changed the headline for this afternoon's edition from the one we did have lined up.'

'Oh yes? Dare one ask, young man, what you had lined up?'

'Really pleased with it, I was! "No Tomorrow for Borrow!"' Frank could tell he looked gutted not to be able to use it.

'After the match last night, the editor said it had to be different.'

'So what can we expect tonight then?'

' "Carpenter Nails Hat-Trick!" isn't very original is it? But it's the best I could do.'

As if recalling what he had come to talk about, the look on his face suddenly became more serious.

'I wondered if you had anything to say about the rumours I've been picking up over the last forty-eight hours that everything's set to change dramatically at Oakhill United?'

'I couldn't possibly comment,' Frank batted back. If he kept quiet, he might hear more about what these 'rumours' were.

Much as he didn't like tittle-tattle, he knew the reporter would have his ear close to the ground.

'Yes, certain sources say a consortium has already put in a bid to take over the club with you fronting things with Bennison?'

'Again, I couldn't possibly comment.'

'I do know one thing though that's definitely going to hit the press sooner or later,' the reporter said, as if determined to stretch out the conversation.

'Oh?'

'Yes one of my colleagues happened to see Councillor Preston, a virtuous married man if ever, smooching with a fancy woman in a coffee-bar in a shopping mall in Manchester. My friend's onto the case!'

'Really?'

'It's not exactly a sports-page story but I know what headline I'd give it . . .'

Frank said nothing.

' "This Could Costa Career!" Witty, don't you think?'

'Hilarious, I'm sure,' replied Frank. 'Now do you mind? Some of us have got proper work to do.'

'You don't mind me contacting you again after the Board meeting?'

'That's what you're paid for isn't it?' And then not wanting to sound too amenable, 'But be a good lad and make it the morning after.'

Frank realised it might look rather strange to Matt Johnson if he started quizzing him too directly about the Skiptons and For Sale signs. So once he had tracked him down, he had started more tentatively by asking him how things were going generally in the Academy.

'Only there's a Board meeting tonight . . . and if I should get asked about how the Academy is faring, I'd like to be able to provide an update.'

'Sorry I haven't wired you a formal report, boss.'

'That's all right. Just let me know verbally.'

After five minutes or so of listening, Frank had interjected, 'Have we managed to keep the same complement of players we started out with?'

Matt had glanced back, slightly puzzled-looking at the question.

'I only ask because, as you know, I live on the same road as Ben Skipton and I saw a For Sale sign up outside his house.'

Not a very subtle approach, admittedly, but it seemed to serve the purpose.

A sudden look of recollection dawned on Matt's face. 'Now you come to mention it, Ben stopped on after training yesterday and we had a long conversation. Actually, he did pretty well all the talking.'

Like mother, like son, Frank rather cruelly thought to himself.

'And?' he was keen to know.

'Yes, Ben says he and his mum are moving out of what he always calls "the hovel". They're going back to live at his dad's. All Ben told me yesterday was that his dad had some awful fall-out with the woman he'd been living with. Mum and dad seem to be back together big-time. The three of them are off on holiday together to Florida soon. According to Ben, mum's even enticed dad to stump up the costs. Ben got quite comical. He said his mum was pushing forty and ancient but she could still charm the birds out of the trees when she wanted to! Or did he say monkeys?'

Matt paused, thinking Frank might laugh but he only grimaced. He quickly resumed his tale in more serious vein. 'I think Ben's main interest in telling me was to let me know he was sorry he would be missing training for two weeks or so. Presumably hoping it wouldn't count against him too much in the meantime.'

Frank thought Matt had finished but the other man clearly had something else he wished to add.

'By the way, I think you can take a hell of a lot of credit yourself, boss.'

'Credit? What for?'

172

'Well, Ben thinks the whole different situation's down to him having shown his parents he could fight his way back into the Academy. He really believes it's the reason why his mum and dad feel hunky-dory about each other again . . . and him! And between the two of us, let's face it, you were the one who strongly advocated him being brought back into the squad.'

Frank couldn't prevent himself shaking his head in bewilderment. At least it helped explain who the man was wining and dining Rosie on the night in question. Her ex-husband! Or rather no longer ex, because he himself, by design or by blunder, had somehow contrived a perfect marital reconciliation. He didn't feel there was much further to discuss with Matt.

'Oh, that's interesting,' was all he managed to say mechanically as he left Matt's office.

'There's still time, you know for me to put something together in the way of a short report on the progress of the squad as a whole, if you like?' Matt called out after him.

'Thanks, but that really will not be necessary,' Frank had concluded. He reckoned he had already been told more than he could cope with.

Frank blinked at the headline in the Friday edition of the Oakhill Times: *OAKHILL UNITED FOOTBALL CLUB IN NEW SHANGRI-LA!* Apart from anything else, it was a good plug for Shazad, the newly-appointed Chair of the Board, not to mention his business empire. Knowing how the reporter's mind worked, he had speculated on other possible ones which could have emerged from the Board meeting. 'No Sorrow for Borrow' came to mind. Wonder where the inspiration for that had come from.

The local reporter had got back to Frank that morning but clearly had bigger fish to fry at that stage in the proceedings. It was Shazad's picture that was blazoned across the front page with some of his other consortium associates. A report of a post-meeting interview with Arnold Preston also caught Frank's eye. He imagined the ex-Chair picking up the rag at the same time as him and cursing the story that he couldn't miss plastered over the whole front page, not to mention the several further column inches inside.

At the Board meeting Arnold had acted like a man facing his own personal Waterloo. Frank wouldn't have been surprised if the reporter had come up with a headline of 'Preston's Last Stand!'.

But the writing was on the wall when it became clear that the ruling from the report was that the club had to find buyers or face an immediate winding-up order. Arnold had apparently struggled behind the scenes to launch some counter-bid to the so-called Shangri-La consortium. But it had been judged far too speculative to warrant consideration. For once, Arnold's finely chiselled words must have fallen on stony ground. Even his staunchest allies on the Board could see the way things were shaping up. In a rearguard action, Arnold had argued that it was dangerous to risk sacrificing the club to a takeover by outsiders who put business interests first. At this point, Shazad had stood up to him impressively:

'My business interest may be in Manchester but I was born and brought up here. I'm Oakhill through and through!' The irony wasn't lost on listeners that this was one of Arnold Preston's own favourite lines.

Shazad continued with a cutting edge of conviction breaking into his voice. 'It really hurts me to admit this, not least because I've been a Board member already for several months. During that time, I've cringed at the lack of proper direction at the club, until very recently, that is.' Here, Shazad had stopped to look meaningfully in Frank's direction before his gaze fell again on Arnold Preston.

'Plus the fact match results never seemed to matter very much. Setting sights any higher was deemed to be setting the club up for a fall. More to the point, Arnold, you've kept everything exactly the way you wanted things to stay. That is, in the doldrums but with everyone having to kowtow to you as Chair.'

As Shazad momentarily paused, there was a deathly hush in the Board room. Were they waiting to see if he had still more to say or whether Arnold Preston would take advantage of the temporary lull to rebut the case being made against him? Frank had expected to hear him, at this point, preach his usual sermon about traditional values but, for once, he didn't seem inclined to peddle the familiar spiel about Oakhill being a family club. Instead, seemingly lost for words, Arnold Preston had only glanced in appeal towards his fellow board members. But looking round the table for support, one after the other they had averted their eyes from him.

This in itself seemed to lend Shazad further momentum. 'Thankfully we're in a position where, for the good of Oakhill United, the present regime is coming to an end. Supporters can look forward to the promise of a new era. I firmly believe our consortium can bring success to the club. We will not only invest resources in Oakhill United to repay the wanton debts that have accumulated in recent times. We will also invest in whatever it takes to gain promotion from League 2 this year. Yes this season: 2010/2011!'

It was as if an unspoken cheer went up through the room. The sense of excitement was palpable. From being an imponderable, there now seemed only one way for Oakhill United to go.

After the consortium bid was formally accepted, Shazad lost no time in announcing that it had been decided Frank and Tony Bennison would form the new management team.

Frank felt a certain sneaking sympathy for Simon Steele in all this. Significantly, he didn't sit next to his revered mentor Preston at the meeting. He too must have sensed what was coming. Admittedly not altogether a kind thought, Frank only hoped Simon's mortgage company would be understanding of his new circumstances. It was difficult to weigh up his chances of getting another job at all quickly.

It had surprised Frank when Arnold had come up to him at the end of the meeting: 'Cracking good win last night. Well done!'

Frank wondered what instinct could be prompting him to say this. Proverbial wild horses wouldn't normally drag a compliment out of him. Unless of course it had been directed Simon's way. With Steele's number up, it was rather late in the day for Preston to be switching tactics.

'Sorry I couldn't make it to the match. It's the first one, home or away, I've missed in years. Pressing alternative engagement.'

Again, Frank let the other man's remark pass. After all, he knew damned well why he had missed the match. It was because he had brought forward the meeting investigating players' complaints against the Executive Manager. That was so he would have ammunition in readiness for the Board meeting. But presumably unbeknown to Arnold, Jed Forrester had made a point of telling Frank after the match on Wednesday night that the players in question had met up themselves. They had not only decided to withdraw complaints but also put on record their support for Frank. It had obviously paid off handsomely losing £150 at the senior pro poker table! Of course, Frank trusted it was more to do with them realising the team had to work harder if they were to obtain good results on the field of play.

Arnold persisted. 'I've always been a great fan of yours Frank. But I have to say it doesn't look like I'm much in favour with this new Board of Directors,' he said like a man-of-the-world knowing he was talking to someone of similar viewpoint. And then in the next breath, 'By the way, do you think you could have a word on my behalf to the new owners to keep me on the Board? In my view the club could still do with someone like myself with political interest . . . er service . . . to protect in the local community.'

Frank couldn't help thinking he had heard Arnold Preston right the first time. 'I'd really love to,' he said back, 'except you know it's not my job as manager to try and determine Board thinking.'

The property they were looking at now was the one Emily preferred out of them all. It was in a pleasant residential area on the outskirts of Oakhill. The first thing she had noticed was that it was set back from the road with a good-sized front garden which gave a more private aspect than others they had visited. Inside, it was not too big for a man living on his own but spacious enough and in very good condition for a house built in the late 1940s. Frank himself had only piped up once during the visit. It was when they had been in the lounge. He had stopped by a space of open wall and uttered cryptically, 'That's good. It could go there!'

Mystified, she had said, 'What could go up there?'

'The next one in the eight-year sequence – the framed picture of the Oakhill United Football Club championship-winning team of 2011!'

God, she thought to herself, if he was now thinking that could happen, anything was possible!

This property wasn't among the six she had picked out for Frank a few weeks back. It had just come on the market. Funnily enough, she had noted that three of those properties that Frank had looked at on his own had since been taken.

Last week had been the most hectic yet. She had been supposing Frank would just be inclined to put his feet up on Sunday but he had primed her to find more properties to look at.

'Do you intend taking the exercise a bit more seriously this time?' she asked cheekily.

'How do you mean?' he said, in surprised tone.

'I even suspected at the time that you didn't darken the door of any of those houses I spent so much time choosing for you to look at.'

'Oh, yes I did!' he protested.

'It's just that you didn't make any comment.' She paused before continuing, 'So this time round, you're a bit keener to leave that dreadful place you live in?'

It seemed strange to think back to that time she had driven onto the estate to meet him to hand over the keys before fleeing as quickly as she could.

'It's not that bad!'

'Tell me one good thing about that house on Queen Anne's Way,' she had pressed.

'I'm afraid I can't,' he had replied but with a look on his face as if he had had to think about it.

'Well, let's see if we can get our act together this time!'

She had thought on Friday morning that he was just meaning again for her to look out the properties for him. But then he had really surprised her by inviting her to go round with him. Even though she wasn't sure how she would feel if he pressed her for advice, she felt flattered he had asked her.

Actually, it had turned out to be the first of two interesting offers that day. The second was when Shazad Ali, the new Chairman, had appointed her the club's Business Manager. Although he hadn't let on too much at the time, she was sure Frank had been the one who had pressed Shazad to make the offer. Much the same way as he had talked her out of going for the job at the local council.

It was as if she had more reason each day to feel grateful to Frank. On a reciprocal basis, it had been touching how grateful he had sounded when she had agreed to look round with him. He had offered to pick her up today and drive round with her acting as the navigator between the various addresses. Fortunately, there hadn't been cause yet to fall out over directions.

Incidentally she hadn't got round to telling him she'd commissioned a local estate agent to put a For Sale board up outside 8 Queen Anne's Way. She was not about to have him changing his mind again! Besides, in her new role as Business Manager she knew that, although the property wouldn't fetch very much, the club could spend the accruing money far more profitably.

'Now I come to think of it,' Frank said at one point, 'I can't remember you asking me how I'd got on looking round last time.'

'At the time, I don't think I would have dared. For days on end, you were like blue touchpaper.'

'Yes, I suppose so.'

Of course she knew it had largely been down to the pressure of his job.

'I'm so glad it was another good result yesterday,' she reminded him and then rather more pointedly, 'Only you'd probably have called it off today if they'd lost.'

Ignoring her jibe, he countered, 'Do you know we're third in the table and right up there in the promotion race? I can see that picture up on the wall already! No hitch whatsoever.'

'That's fantastic!' She had never heard him sounding so confident. He appeared capable of anything.

After they had visited the last house, he seemed in no hurry to whizz her back home.

'Do you fancy a glass of wine?' he asked her. 'Only it'd be nice to talk over what we've seen. That is, if you've the time to spare . . . I really would appreciate that.'

Giving it a moment's thought, she smiled back. 'Yes. That would be very nice, Frank.'